~~(UN)~~ FORGIVEN
Healing Through the Finished Work of the Cross

Lindy Schlabach

TRILOGY
A WHOLLY OWNED SUBSIDIARY OF TBN

PROFESSIONAL PUBLISHING MEETS POWERFUL PROMOTION

Trilogy Christian Publishers

A Wholly Owned Subsidiary of Trinity Broadcasting Network

2442 Michelle Drive

Tustin, CA 92780

Copyright © 2024 by Lindy Schlabach

Scripture quotations are taken from the Holy Bible, New Living Translation, copyright © 1996, 2004, 2015 by Tyndale House Foundation. Used by permission of Tyndale House Publishers, Inc., Carol Stream, Illinois 60188. All rights reserved.

All rights reserved, including the right to reproduce this book or portions thereof in any form whatsoever.

For information, address Trilogy Christian Publishing

Rights Department, 2442 Michelle Drive, Tustin, CA 92780.

Trilogy Christian Publishing/ TBN and colophon are trademarks of Trinity Broadcasting Network.

For information about special discounts for bulk purchases, please contact Trilogy Christian Publishing.

Trilogy Disclaimer: The views and content expressed in this book are those of the author and may not necessarily reflect the views and doctrine of Trilogy Christian Publishing or the Trinity Broadcasting Network.

10 9 8 7 6 5 4 3 2 1

Library of Congress Cataloging-in-Publication Data is available.

ISBN 979-8-89333-523-1

ISBN (ebook) 979-8-89333-524-8

Dedication

To Pamela and her servant heart; God loves you and so do I.

To my handsome and supportive husband, thank you for loving me as I am.

To my Fit & Funky Workout family, I wouldn't be here without you.

And to my gram, my biggest fan and cheerleader, thank you for loving me when I was unlovable and seeing in me what I couldn't see in myself.

To Alika and Alija, Auntie loves you more than I could ever put into words. You will always be Auntie's nuggets and I am so very proud of who you are.

Foreword by Ben Stuckey

Lindy, The Listener

Lindy Schlabach is a lot of things. Relationally, she's a wife, a daughter, sister, aunt, and a friend. Professionally, Lindy is a life coach and business owner. Spiritually, she is a child of God. Personality-wise, she's loud, comfortable in her own skin, and funny. Moreover, she is a trauma survivor, who has battled obesity, infertility, and sexual assault. But the thing I want to point out, above all else, to you as you read: Lindy is a listener.

Her husband may be the one person to challenge this observation, but I still attest to this superhuman sense Lindy possesses.

Please allow me a few short minutes to explain.

There are few people in this world where I can remember almost every detail from the first time I met them. Lindy Schlabach is on that short list.

Good Friday, 2016, I was finishing up a community worship service at the United Methodist Church in LaGrange, Indiana. This was a service that included many pastors in the community. So when I looked at a crowd and saw a sea of unknown faces it didn't seem odd to me at the time.

As the service ended and people were milling around, a young woman walked up to me and confidently said, "My name is Lindy Miller and I wanted to tell you how much I appreciate your sermons."

Shocked that I didn't know who she was (Lindy doesn't exactly have the LaGrange Vibe) I sheepishly responded, "Thanks. I wish more people would introduce themself as boldly as you did so I didn't have to smile and guess who they are."

And Lindy's next response was what endeared me to her: "I know, you said that in your sermon last week."

For some reason, I was shocked someone was actually listening to what I was saying in my sermons!

But that's the kind of person Lindy truly is, despite what her

(Un) Forgiven

husband may say. For all her confidence and big personality, Lindy is someone who listens! It's her superpower.

Obviously, if you're reading this then you are wanting to listen to Lindy, so you might wonder if you are not experiencing her great strength. But this book is way more than a testimony and devotional. It's a tool Lindy has created to teach you her superb listening skills.

As Lindy tells her story in the first part of the book, you will be the listener.

Don't worry, you won't get bored!

Her transparent storytelling spins hard and fast. In one sentence she will tell you about her flute- playing high school identity. And then one sentence later she is talking about smoking a joint and drinking vodka on the school bus.

Colorfully, she weaves together the patchwork of experiences in her life to create a coat of many colors that would make Joseph, son of Jacob, jealous. Also, like the Joseph narratives in the Old Testament, she will talk about her ups and downs of life. Her testimony of rape, betrayal, infertility, and loneliness will connect with the deep sorrows in your life. But, by the end, you cannot help but be inspired by the resolve in her faith that gives her to strength to say, "What you meant for evil, God meant for good" (Genesis 50:20 NIV).

I guarantee you will be inspired by her journey of healing. I am not just saying this as her former pastor and friend. I am saying this as someone who has walked with her though the valleys in her life. And I have walked with her though the mountaintops. It was during those times where I witnessed this brash woman of God learn to shut up and listen. Listen to the guidance of the Holy Spirit spoken though His Word, His people, and His presence.

By the end of part one you, will be primed to begin your journey of healing. You'll want what Lindy's got: "Ears to hear" – (Matthew 13:16 NIV).

Part Two of the book is where Lindy teaches you her superpower. Lindy will teach you to develop your listening ability.

Lindy Schlabach

The format is simple. It's laid out in daily meditations, guided by God's Word, and Lindy will ask you questions. Sometimes the questions are simple and benign. And some questions punch you in your soul. But, in all ways you will be challenged to become a listener to the Holy Spirit.

You may feel far from God and think you can't hear Him. But He can hear you. If you trust the process, you too will learn to listen.

My friend, I want to challenge you to learn to flex your listening muscle. Go into this book looking to develop a skill long since forgotten. The Bible says, "The path of the righteous is like the first light of dawn, and shines ever brighter until the full light of day" (Proverbs 4:18 NIV).

The short interpretation of this means: Every day gets brighter! I understand if it doesn't seem like it in your life right now. However, if you learn to listen to the whispers and shouts of God's voice, you will gain perspective that will help you discern the twists and turns of your path.

My friend, Lindy, is trustworthy. Allow her to walk at your side, as you begin to create your ~~(Un)~~ *Forgiven* story. Start your journey today and choose the hard path to healing with a little help and encouragement from your new friend

Preface

Abandonment. Rape. Infertility. Drugs and alcohol. Sexual sin, depression, anxiety, gaining 100 pounds, devastating loss and trauma. These are all part of my journey, but they're not who I am anymore. I have dug myself out of the trenches and have found myself set apart because of the love, grace, and mercy of Jesus Christ.

These things may have happened to me, but they do not define me. This book is my testimony, the culmination of my experiences, hurts and my hope, how He met me in my mess, loved me through it, and called me to share my story with you.

Isaiah 43:19 NLT reads, "For I am about to do something new. See, I have already begun! Do you not see it?

I will make a pathway through the wilderness. I will create rivers in the dry wasteland."

I was the wilderness, I was the dry wasteland, until I finally let go and let Him do the work in me that only He could do.

I couldn't do it on my own; I never could, even though I tried. My hope is that you'll be open and honest and real about your journey, your hopes and dreams and healing. He is waiting to meet you too; He has big plans for your life.

I will always struggle to share these parts of my story; they flood back to the surface and bring feelings and thoughts I don't want to relive. Healing is messy; it hurts and is often a daily choice to push forward, one seemingly small step at a time.

If I could ask one thing as you read through the devotional part of this book, it would be to take your time. Be in tune with the Holy Spirit and ask Him to reveal Himself to you in a mighty way. You are never too far from His graces; you are worthy of healing and hope and change. Let His truth take root in your heart and you will be transformed in a way that can only be described as the workings of the One who created you before Genesis one.

Acknowledgments

I would like to thank my husband, Darrel. Without you this book would still be on my computer and in my heart. Thank you for believing in me and investing in these words. To Ben Stuckey, for pushing me all those years ago to face my past, lean on God's Word for healing and truth and to study scripture and seek answers for myself. Thank you for being boldly you, for your unwavering friendship and support to Darrel and me in our many adventures in this life. To my friends, for always loving me as I am, for listening and praying for these words, for always being there for every part of my life, big and small. Praise be to God, the Healer and Deliverer of my life. Your grace, love, mercy, and blessings continue to follow me through every day. I am here, Lord, Your faithful servant, send me wherever You may. I may not be ready, but I am willing. To Tricia and TBN for taking a chance on this book, I am forever grateful.

~~(Un)~~ Forgiven

Introduction

My life has been a series of messes, mostly at my own hand. This book is my testimony. These words, while not always easy to share, show the real, raw, and honest struggle of my life. It has been a decade of conviction to write, but a decade of fear of the truth and the hurt and putting myself out there in the most vulnerable sense.

It is my hope that as you read this book, you will take some of the teachings that have helped me work through the trials and struggles in my life and use them to help yourself, however that may look, as you continue or begin your own healing journey.

Many of the principles that have shaped me, I've learned from amazing people who have been courageous enough to share their personal struggles and triumphs over the past. Some offer tangible steps that I've been able to incorporate into my life to create a habit of self-discipline I never knew I had or even wanted.

Self-discipline is a fruit of the Spirit, so if you have Jesus in your heart, you have it; you may just need to cultivate it a bit. I know I had to. Maybe you don't know the story of Jesus but you're searching for something, and you were led to these words. First, let me say thank you for the opportunity to share with you.

While I've read countless self-help books over the years, many faith-based, the most influential book in my life has been the Bible. When I started reading it in 2017, I honestly didn't expect much, if I'm being honest. I guess I should say, I didn't expect that it would change me as it did. I didn't quite grasp the messy people who fought to bring us the Word, I figured that the people we sang about in Sunday School all had the happy-go-lucky lives that went along to the beat of the music. I found that this is not the case. I found comfort in the failings of Adam and Eve and their kids, Cain and Abel, Moses and Aaron, King David, Saul, and Solomon. I resonated with Peter and Matthew and even found a little Judas in my heart at times.

My healing journey began as a quest to lose weight after gaining 100 pounds, but it became so much more. It brought me back to God, who brought me back to life. It has been a curvy, topsy-turvy journey, with highs and lows and in between. It has brought the worst of times through loss and trauma and infertility, but it's also given me HOPE. I didn't feel worthy. I didn't feel redeemable. I didn't feel like my life was important or valued. I felt like my sin was too big and that God was ashamed of me. Then I read His Word; I let it sink into the depths of my aching, broken heart. Verse by verse, word by word, promise by promise, He began to bring beauty from the ashes I thought had been whisked away. No matter how far you've fallen away from Him, maybe you've never met Him at all, let me be very clear here, He loves you, He is FOR you, you ARE worthy. You are not a mistake. Your life has purpose, and no matter how alone or broken you feel, you are redeemable. You are chosen. You are (~~Un~~)-Forgiven.

Table of Contents

Dedication i
Foreword by Ben Stuckey ii
Preface v
Acknowledgments vi
Introduction vii
Prologue x
My Testimony 2
My Story 10
The Call 12
The Gift 14
The Lesson 16
Who Are You? 18
We Are His 20
Fruit 23
The Plan 25
Discipline 28
Trust 31
Boundaries 33
Spiritual Discipline 36
Prayer 38
Be Encouraged! 41
A Final Thought and Call to Action 162
Appendix 165
Notes 167
About the Author 169

Prologue

How do you quiet the noise? How do you stay focused and determined in your faith walk? How do you, with faith, show up on the days you'd rather shove your head in the sand? Well, I'm not sure, beyond saying "Give it to God and trust." It sounds easy, doesn't it? Oh, yeah, just give it to God, girl.... First off, not everyone knows just HOW to do that. If you're a woman, you're probably a control freak or maybe a "reformed" one. We want to know, "When will I find 'the one?' When will my life make sense? When will I lose weight? When will I ...." Fill in your blanks.

One thing I know is God's time isn't our time. Another thing I know is that you're not going to get all your prayers answered until you're well and ready to handle the responsibility required to manage the task at hand. For years I've been saying I want to build a seven figure a year business. Okay, but why? My answer used to be of the world; today I say, "I want to earn a million dollars a year and give it all away. I want to live on 20 % of our income and bless those who have blessed me." Today, my prayer has become, "Thy will, not my will, be done." Truth be told, our income doesn't determine our success, I truly believe that honoring God with our choices and learning to discern the voice of the Holy Spirit, then living by that conviction, is the TRUE measure of success. "Thy will be done" is the hardest prayer I've ever prayed, and I first really began to pray it as I was going through my infertility journey. I always wanted to be a mom; I dreamed of a large family. I grew up surrounded by aunts and uncles and cousins and I wanted that for my kids. Two years, medical menopause, multiple procedures, and 18 months of hemorrhaging, I still ended up having a hysterectomy. I was devastated, I felt broken and unworthy; woman was created to create and once again, I had failed. In true God fashion, how-

~~(Un)~~ Forgiven

ever, He delivered me from my shame and reminded me who His Word says I am, worthy, beautiful, strong, and fearfully and wonderfully made. What sort of mess are you finding yourself in today? Where have you felt lost in your life's journey? Do you truly believe, without a doubt, that God loves you and cares for you and is deeply intertwined in the details of your life? He is there; He is with you.

I first felt I should write a book about 15 years ago. I started it and stopped, because I wasn't sure I could share the truth of this life of mine and be completely fine with what it would bring. Today, after four decades of life, I've learned that He knows best and that ache will always be there until I continue to forge forward, leaning on Him for assurance and guidance to the next step. Are you willing to forget everything about who you think you should be and step into the path and purpose that was created for you before the Earth was formed? I hope so. I need you; the world needs you; YOU need you to be all you were created to be. Stop living in fear, stop selling yourself short. Trust and believe that where God guides, He more than provides.

This book is a testimony of what He has done and continues to do in my life. I hope you start to talk to Him, to let Him change you, shape you and mold you. Open yourself to Him and watch Him bring beauty from your ashes. We can hide our messes, try to control the outcomes, or trust that His ways are better. We've tried to control long enough; we never had control anyway. The second you decide that you're done living up to others' expectations of you and step into the promise and the future of the Creator of all things, that is when you start to live the life He meant for you, loving and serving others, confident in the fact that you were created exactly as you are so you can exactly who you are called to be.

My Testimony

I grew up with a fairly normal childhood. My parents divorced when I was three, but both sides of my family have always been close. I spent a lot of time with both sets of grandparents because my mom worked so much to support us. My dad moved to Tennessee when they divorced, so I spent a month each summer with him. He remarried when I was eight. They both struggled with alcohol and drug addiction; it was hard to be there, if I'm being honest. She never seemed to want me around. I remember one vacation my grandparents had taken us on, my aunt overheard my stepmom tell people they'd met that they "didn't have any kids." That pretty much sums up how I felt during summers there. Their son, my brother Jimmy, is almost 18 years my junior. At home, things were good. My mom remarried also, and I had a little brother when I was 10. Jevon and his wife have two kids and my husband, who grew up Amish, has 21 nieces and nephews. We are busy between our two families. My brother and sister-in-law let us have the nuggets any time we ask. It wasn't perfect, but I loved our life. My dad moved back to the area when I was in middle school; we had a rocky relationship until I was in my mid-thirties because of his addiction. Two months before I graduated high school, my youngest brother Jimmy was born. I was in the room when he was born; it was one of the most beautiful things I have ever experienced. Once he was born, I looked forward to spending time there.

I was always active as a kid; I was a competitive dancer for ten years and we traveled all over the country dancing and competing, it kept me busy, and I learned a good deal about discipline at a young age. I played sports through middle school and played the flute in the high school marching band until I graduated.

I remember smoking my first joint out of a dollar bill when I was 14. I drank vodka on the school bus not long after that. I

(Un) Forgiven

remember the slow walk home after I'd been caught at school, thinking that my mom would killlll me... I was grounded indefinitely and almost expelled; she had to hire a lawyer to keep me in school. It was not a good time in my life. Thankfully, not long after that a friend invited me to his Wednesday night youth group at the church down the street. I'd found home. I was saved at youth conference that summer and I can still remember how the Holy Spirit spoke to me in that moment, the feeling of warmth running through my body and the feeling that I'd never again be alone. I was high on Jesus, and it felt SO good.

I had a good group of friends in high school, and I loved it, but I couldn't wait to go to college. After graduation I attended a private Christian University a couple hours from home; it was amazing! My own schedule, boys, FREEDOM, boys. I started hanging with the party crowd; I was getting drunk and high any time I could. The summer before my senior year, I was raped. I was at a friend's party, drunk and high. I asked him if I could sleep in his bed and woke up to him having sex with me in the middle of the night. I told him no and to get off me, over and over, until eventually, he did. I was so drunk I rolled over and passed out. I woke up the next morning full of shame in search of my underwear, leaving them somewhere in the pit of that room. I went home sobbing and told my roommate what had happened. She looked me square in the eyes and said, "What do you expect? You were drunk and slept in his bed." The boy was my friend; I expected kindness, not trauma. He'd spent time with me in my hometown, my parents had taken him to dinner, he was like a brother to me, and my roommate, my supposed friend, sent me straight to hell with her condemnation. I felt shame, and for 15 years I stayed silent about my abuse. Within 12 months of my assault, I was diagnosed with anxiety and depression and placed on medication. I should have talked to someone. I gained 100 pounds in my suffering. He was wrong. My roommate was wrong. It wasn't my fault. I needed someone to tell me that. I'm telling you now, it isn't your fault, it wasn't your fault. If you've experienced any kind of trauma in your life, you didn't deserve it, but you DO deserve to heal.

I'd pushed my trauma down SO far, that until 2017, I'd forgotten what had happened to me. That sounds crazy, I know. Of course, a lot had happened in the 15 years before, and I'll share bits as we move forward, but the point I want you to understand is that no matter where you've found yourself in life, God is there for you. In an instant, you can turn to Him, talk to Him, even if you never have before, and He will show Himself to you. He did it for me in 1996 and in 2016 and He will for you today. Just say His name.

In 2017 I decided to invest in a network marketing company and one of our daily habits is personal development. As I was reading *Breaking Free* by Beth Moore, the memories returned, the sights and smells of that terrible basement bedroom returned, and I cried out to God to forgive me. It was then that my healing process began. I started the book hoping to forgive my dad for his addiction and all the hurt he'd put me through, and to work through my crappy relationship habits in hopes of someday having a relationship that wasn't based on sex or a high. How are you supposed to heal and forgive yourself after 15 years of drug and alcohol abuse and sexual promiscuity? How are you supposed to forgive someone who takes something from you that is so personal? How do we quiet the lies of the enemy who seeks to destroy us? We seek God's Word, we find His grace, we repent, we accept His mercy and bask in His truth and peace.

I had to forgive my rapist, I had to forgive my roommate, I had to forgive myself. And that took time. God taught me in that moment that we all fall short of His glory, hat I was a sinner too and that if I needed forgiveness then I had to give it to those who had hurt me, ALL of them. I forgave my rapist. I forgave my roommate. Most importantly, I forgave myself. You MUST forgive yourself too. My roommate had me convinced in that moment that I had "asked for it" that I "deserved it." Those are lies straight from the pit of hell, and we MUST fight the evil forces that wage war in our mind.

Despite my struggles that were mostly self-inflicted, my life has been blessed. I was raised by my mom with lots of help from my grandparents after my dad moved when my parents divorced. My grandparents spoiled me, our family traveled all over. I grew up in church and was always going with either of my grandpar-

~~(Un)~~ Forgiven

ents and mom if she wasn't working. I am a very blessed woman who happens to have survived some hurts along the way, many because of my poor choices and abandoning God. Thankfully, He never abandoned me, and after years of searching, I found my home and hope in Christ. I am forgiven. I hope this book is a testament to that and a reminder that no matter where you've found yourself in life, that He IS the living hope, our comfort and shield. I hope that my story encourages you and helps you, not only to seek Him daily, but to step out in faith and purpose and to heal in any way you need it. I've included applicable steps along with daily verses to keep you encouraged. I hope this can be a safe place for you to connect with God in an intimate way and seek His will above all else. The world is noisy; there are so many false truths out there. Let me put this as clear as I can; Jesus loves you; He died and rose again so that you could know Him and His love, grace, mercy, and forgiveness. Share Him, shine boldly and brightly, bringing glory to Him in all you do, and let Him shine through you in a way only He can.

By His grace alone, I am free. I am not ashamed. I am worthy. I am *(Un)-Forgiven.*

And so, my friend, are you.

After college, I moved home to bartend and was quickly promoted to full-time. I was drinking most days and when I wasn't bartending, I was sitting on the other side, gambling, drinking, and picking up the occasional man. My life for 15 years was partying; I made many poor choices with men, food, alcohol, and drugs. Over the course of the next few years, I gained 50 pounds. In 2008 my world came to a crashing halt; my grandpa was diagnosed with stage 4 pancreatic cancer. He was my everything; my world was falling apart. I'll share more on this later, but after his death I lay on the couch for 13 months, gaining another 50 pounds, finding comfort in anything I could that wasn't good for me. One day in 2009 it was like God reached down from heaven and pulled me off that couch. I decided that day to take control of my weight. Of course, I did it all wrong; I went from fad diet to fad diet, keto and South Beach, to everything in between. If there was a pill, diet, ab rocket or soup that promised weight loss, I bought it. I managed to get a bit of weight off over time, but I was still making poor choices every weekend. I'd lose a pound or two Monday-Thursday and gain it back every weekend…the endless cycle of defeat. I started hanging out with the Witmer Lake crowd and wow did the partying take a drastic step up, or down, I guess depending on how you looked at it. I was in a very unhealthy friendship with someone who only wanted to be friends on her terms. Over time it became exhausting and after a few years, I'd had enough. After a disastrous girls' trip to Florida, I walked away. Three weeks before that trip, a friend who would later be my matron of honor invited me to church. God had His hand on me.

I was back home where there were no conditions on love; I found His peace and all that it brings. I hadn't been to church consistently since I was in high school, besides the occasional Easter service with my grandma. That day, I heard a pastor that changed the way I looked at Jesus. He talked about relationship, not religion. I rededicated my life back to Jesus about a month later in my car driving to work, listening to a local radio station. I bawled my eyes out, I let it all go. My past, my rapist, my father who'd been absent and addicted for most of my life, my unkind friend, I let it all go. I poured it all out to God and something in my heart started to shift. He began a new work in me, and some of that is what I hope to share with you through this book.

In 2016 my friend and I started doing at-home workouts. We'd been going to the gym, but our work schedules changed, and we needed something we could do at home, so she came over every day for 90 days and we worked out in my living room. It was awesome! After I completed my program, my coach invited me to learn about earning income from sharing my workouts and helping people find the success I had. I hadn't even lost an ounce, but I *had* finished something hard for the first time in a long time. I was leery, but I prayed over it. A few months later I dove deep into coaching and my life will never be the same. Once I really started to dig into the programs, I realized the value of pairing 30-minute workouts with simply laid out nutrition. I lost seven pounds in two weeks eating more food than ever and

~~(Un)~~ Forgiven

I *knew* I was in the right place.

One of our daily coaching activities is personal development. I found myself reading books in my home library that would help develop my faith; I committed to reading and really studying the Bible.

Three months after committing to this business I was faced with my rape and all the hurt it brought. For 15 years I'd pushed it down deep and as I started to read and pray, I realized that the year before my fitness journey began, my rapist reached out to me to reconnect. Wow, it took some serious inner healing, as I mentioned before, but by the grace of God through Holy Spirit connection, this community of women I get to immerse myself in daily, and through a physical desire to change, God has done such an incredible work in my life.

The next year I got laid off and my little brother got shot. He is okay, but it was traumatic for him and for our family. I spent most of that summer helping him rehab in Florida. I came home a few months later and started hemorrhaging, which I have come to realize was from the stress my body underwent. After almost two years of surgeries and medical menopause, I had a hysterectomy in 2020 and in my pit, my hurt, my loneliness and despair, God delivered my future husband next door, just as I'd prayed. As I sit here typing, he is snoozing on the couch. We're heading to our discipleship group here in a few minutes and as I sit here in gratitude for all God has done, is doing and all He will do, I can't wait to see what He does next. I don't know what the future will bring, but I *do* know that God has never left me, and He will never leave you.

He is always waiting, even in your mess, for you to come home. There's a beautiful image floating around social media titled "When I arrive in heaven" and it's Jesus hugging a woman and she is beaming from ear to ear. That is the hope we all have when our anchor is found in His precious love. My prayer is that you are blessed by these words, that you will tuck a scripture in your heart as you prepare for this journey and be open to the work He will do through these words. This book is my testimony, the good, the bad, the ugly, the celebration and everything in between. Just remember that you are free, you are worthy, and you *are* (~~UN~~)-FORGIVEN.

In 2008, we lost my grandpa; it was awful, the worst year of my life. People talk about the economic crash; I don't remember that. I do remember being on spring break with my family in Florida and Gram called to tell us it was stage 4 and he had months to live. I was shattered. Grandpa Jim was my guy. He taught me to ride a bike, how to swim, he inspired me to want to be successful in my life, to cherish my family, among many other things. The thought of living without him was unbearable to me; it became my mission to see that his last days on this earth were peaceful. He was diagnosed in April and passed August 1st; I am so glad I got those last few months with him. The day he died, I was getting ready to go get my hair cut. Gram came in to tell me she thought "this was it." He'd been in a coma for almost two weeks; his mouth had been open and he was breathing this loud breath most of the time. So, after he finally passed, I tried to close his mouth, but it wouldn't budge. We were standing around the end of his bed, my Aunt Sis and I chatting while we were rubbing his legs, and my great aunt came in from calling her daughter to tell her the news and said, "WHO DID THAT TO HIS FACE?" He was grinning from ear to ear; it makes me tear up every time I think about it. I will NEVER forget the look on his face. I knew then that heaven was real, and God had him. Even still, as mentioned earlier, I fell into a pit of depression for 13 months after he died and ended up 100 pounds overweight.

Fast forward ten years later, April 7th, 2018, when our family faced another tragedy. While I won't get into the specifics, it caused my dad to get sober. It was a shock to all of us, and while no one's life ended, yet another miracle, it was enough to scare my dad into sobriety. He went to rehab, got saved, and walked me down the aisle when hubs and I got married, something I'd prayed for years but honestly had given up hope for. God brought beauty from our ashes.

Do you know what "omnipresent" means? It means that God is everywhere, all the time! The devil is not. Yes, there is a devil; scripture tells us he prowls around seeking to DESTROY you. He hates you and he wants you to hate yourself, so you'll shame

~~(Un)~~ Forgiven

yourself into fear and doubt yourself, keeping you from God's plan. But he is weak, and he isn't omnipresent, which is why he can't be everywhere all the time and he doesn't know your thoughts as God does. I think sometimes we give him too much power. He picks up on the things you say out loud. The POWER of your words is so important. When you say something negative about yourself or someone else, the devil and his evil cohorts are right there to take those words and spit them back to you when you're in a cycle of negativity or feeling defeated. We MUST change the words that come out of our mouths; we must change the actions we take. The Bible tells us that we must "take every thought captive and make it obedient to Christ." (2 Corinthians 10:5 NLT.) Sometimes the negativity we face is our own self-talk, sometimes it's from the past, someone who hurt us or made us feel bad, sometimes it's the enemy. We MUST take those thoughts captive and turn them over to Jesus. Let His truth sink into the depths of your heart.

My Story

After I came home from helping my brother rehab in 2018, I started hemorrhaging from the stress. As I mentioned previously, multiple surgeries led to medical menopause and eventually, 18 months later, a hysterectomy. I was shattered. Who would want a 36-year-old barren woman with a sketchy past and ruined body? My sexual past was coming back to haunt me; years of using sex as a weapon turned on me. I would never find happiness; this was the lie I started to believe. For years I'd done online dating off and on and given up hope. I started to pray, big BOLD prayers. "Lord, I can't online date anymore, can you please just place my future husband in front of my car or let him move in next door? I am tired, I am alone, I am fulfilled but I want more in this life, I want to share it with someone." I used to have a long list of "must haves" in men, but it came down to: he must love God and have a job. That February in 2020, the man who would be my husband moved in next door. Only God. And not only did he have those two qualities, but he also had many of the others I'd always hoped for, and many I didn't know I needed in my life. The craziest part of all of this is that we know so many of the same people and have hung out in the same places, but never met. God knew when our time would be, and He made it happen. Marriage isn't easy; it takes loads of patience and self-sacrifice, but it is a way to honor God and one I am so grateful to do with such an incredible man.

He WILL answer your prayer, He WILL move your mountain. But you must not only believe, but KNOW that He will. Know that it won't be on your timeline or usually how you imagine it. It'll be better, it'll be perfect, and when it's of God, you know it'll be forever. Just like writing this book. I pray over the words; I pray over the message. I want you to read this book and be inspired to connect with Him in a way you never have before. I want you to remember the stories of the hot messes in the Bible who were used to do GREAT things for the Kingdom of God, and to own your mess and step into the greatness He has planned for you. You will fall, you will question, you will want to quit. Please don't. Lean in, let Him lead, and watch how He transforms your life in a way you never knew was possible. But how?

If you're a new believer, the devil will come at you hard. Stay in faith, don't lose hope, surround yourself with fellow believers who will help cover you. Pray out loud, WORSHIP out LOUD! When you wake up with worship in your head, Satan flees; when you speak Jesus out of your mouth, the enemy flees.

Bad things will always happen, scripture tells us that. Eve ate from the tree of knowledge of good and evil and sin entered our lives. Scripture promises that we will have bad things happen. "In this world you WILL have trouble but take heart! I have overcome the world." (John 16:33) He has overcome! God doesn't cause bad to happen, but He does allow it because He wants us to come to Him when we are burdened, and He wants His name to be glorified in your struggle. We can't do life without Him, and we shouldn't try to. "His ways are higher than our ways, His thoughts are not our thoughts." (Isaiah 55:8) Wouldn't you rather not face the headache of having to control everything, when the God of the universe wants to act on your behalf?

The Call

Sometimes the places you go and the things you feel called to aren't anywhere near where you thought you'd be or end up... do you have that blind faith? Do you trust that God is moving in you and will take you where you need to go? Are you willing and able to lay down your life to live only for Him and not the plans you've made for your life?

You must believe that no matter where you find yourself God's plans will always be better than your own. And as hard as it can be to let go of control, if you truly want to live His best for your life, you've got to move into complete and total faith and belief that if you have a plan and a purpose for your life He will move you to it.

When you think of your failures or the things in your past you've yet to face, how do they make you feel? Why do you think you hold on to those thoughts of shame and unforgiveness for yourself? You've got to dig deep into your faith and cry out to God to take those things from you. You've got to get down on your knees and let it go; He's forgiven you, it's time to forgive yourself. God wants to take it from you, He wants all of you; the good, the bad, the truly ugly, and everything in between. He loves you, yes, even the ugly stuff. You must forgive yourself; you MUST forgive those people in your past that you don't want to. You're holding on to something that you don't need to hold on to and you've got to, for YOUR sake, let it go.

(UN)-Forgiven is NOT a life to live. You are lovable. You ARE worthy. You ARE loved by the God who created the universe, every bird, every bug, every sparrow. God cares about all of them; why for a second do you think He wouldn't care about you? HE DOES. But to receive His forgiveness, you must first offer it to those who are sometimes undeserving. We are ALL undeserving, but He hands it out anyway. We were destined for hell, yet His death took that shame and through repentance and forgiveness we are saved!

Find a group of God-loving people who are on the same path as you, maybe a few are ahead of the curve, maybe some behind you, but either way, we need other believers to speak life and truth into us, every day, yes, but especially on the days we're not sure how we'll make it through. Do you have people in your life like that? I hope so. Are you that someone in another believer's life? I hope you strive for that. We are better together; we are meant to be together. Scripture tells us that "Where two or three are gathered in my name, I am there." (Matthew 18:20) Find your people. Seek out people to fill you, sustain you and build you up when you need it. But we must BE a friend to have a friend. We need to be a friend first; reach out to people and ask how you can pray for them. Prayer is the best gift you can give another human being; prayer changes the world. YOU CAN CHANGE THE WORLD. One prayer, one moment, one choice to pour into another believer's life, or unbeliever for that matter. Prayer is what it takes to make a difference. Do it once, then do it again. Ghandhi said, "Be the change you wish to see in the world." Do you believe that you can make a difference? Do you KNOW that you can make a difference? Because you CAN. My friend! Beloved! You were created for a purpose and the world needs you to own it.

The Gift

Let's talk about forgiveness. Who do you need to forgive? I've been bullied more as an adult than I ever was in school. And it SUCKS. I'm soft hearted, I'm non-confrontational, and quite honestly, I'm just not going to let someone steal my peace. The more I talk to women everywhere, it blows me away the struggles they have with relationships in their family. When I was dealing with everything with my brother a few years back, my cousin said something to me that always stuck. She said, "He knows you love him unconditionally and will do anything for him. You're his safe space to lash out, knowing he can always come to you." Have you ever experienced this with a loved one? I've experienced it with more than a few. It hurts. At my age, what I allow is different; there's a difference between being a doormat and someone your loved one needs in times of trouble. We've all been unlovable, so let's keep that in perspective. We have all sinned and fallen short of God's glory; we're human. And as we've talked about before, when you have Jesus in your life, you have the fruits of the Spirit, but you also have those fleshy parts of you that wage war between good and evil. Learn to listen to the Spirit's prompting, learn to lean away from your flesh and not buy into your sometimes fickle feelings. You are made to live for Christ and HIS will for your life; we are called to serve.

It occurred to me recently, while I was out to eat, how much time we actually have to give. I was watching people drinking and socializing, and not to say that's a bad thing, in moderation of course, but what if we used half the time we go to dinner or sit at the bar or in front of the TV to volunteer somewhere or give back our time? What if we, instead, used it to make someone's life better? You don't have to give money; you can give time. You don't have to give time; you can give money. You can spend

(Un)-Forgiven

time in prayer, lifting up people specifically in hurtful situations or lost people in general. There are so MANY ways to give back, and I think that if we try, we could see how many opportunities there actually ARE to do something good for someone else. If God came back right now, what would you be doing?

I'm reading a Bible study with a friend online; she's dealing with some pretty heavy anxiety and today our study said, "If you could see Jesus standing beside you right now, do you think you would be afraid of anything?" WOW! That is an incredible thought for ANY of us to fathom! Can you picture it? Well, guess what, beloved, He IS standing right beside you, He is IN you. Will you take a moment and acknowledge the Holy Spirit's presence right now? Go ahead, I'll wait.

We've been talking a lot this week in our workout group about forgiveness. Who do we need to forgive? Someone from our past? Someone from our present? Ourselves? Oftentimes we cannot heal because we've buried a seed so deep in our hearts, we don't even remember WHY we hurt. Will you pray over that seed in your life today? Will you have the courage to allow God to dig it up so you can move on to healing? Will you picture Him standing beside you right now as you strap on your armor and get to work? Forgiveness is hard work. Oftentimes we're offering it to someone who either doesn't deserve it, who has died, or we don't know how or even want to contact them. Forgiveness isn't for them, it's for you. So, if you are the one you're punishing from past hurts, I ask you now to get to your knees and ask God to reveal your trauma, to release your trauma, and that you can work now on the healing part. That takes work. Sometimes it's work repeatedly, because that fleshy part of us wants to pick it back up even when God has taken it, blessed it, and released it. Will you have the courage to "give it up" to God today?

The Lesson

I remember singing songs in Sunday School about Zacchaeus being in a tree. I remember singing about Jonah and the whale, but I don't remember the stories of Zacchaeus being hated and Jonah running from God, like running SO far it'd be like me running to Italy from Indiana.

I wish we'd have learned about David and Bathsheba, not just that he stole and impregnated another man's wife, but that he had that man murdered. I wish we'd have read about what a weirdo John the Baptist was or Noah being a drunk, Moses questioning the audible voice of God, and Abraham and Sarah setting the world up for failure with the birth of Ishmael. How about Peter, who knew Jesus personally yet denied Him three times, or Thomas who questioned everything. These are the people who made HISTORY; they are the reason we have Christianity today. Each of them were messed up sinners who sometimes did horrible things, yet God still used them to move mountains and make a way. Think of Saul, turned Paul, who was seeking out and KILLING Christians thinking he was doing God's work.... Blinded and radically SAVED, becoming one of the leaders in Christ's church. King Soloman, the wisest man ever to ever live, had a drove of concubines, 300 we're told, and 700 wives. It was their pagan gods that eventually ruined Solomon's reign. Yet God still used each of these to do His work; they were forgiven, and you are too if you believe Jesus is the Son of God, and that He died and rose to life for you. Will you receive the gift of salvation today?

Many years ago, our pastor encouraged us to read the Bible for ourselves, and to pray over it; not to just rely on his Sunday sermons but to let God speak to us through His Word. I believe that if it takes two years to read one chapter, but you understand it and apply it to your life, He would rather that than have you

~~(Un)~~ Forgiven

skimming page to page just to say you read it. The Bible is the rule book for our lives; every story is as relevant and applicable today as it was when it was written, some parts over 2,000 years ago. If you need help with disciplining with your kids, struggles in your marriage or job, search and pray over your Bible and ask Him to reveal to you the places to read. Then read it, pray over it, journal how you can apply it, and maybe two or three steps you'll apply that day. Remember, it's the APPLICATION of knowledge that has POWER!

We overcomplicate God so much; it's quite disturbing when I think back to my childhood of all the things I "thought" I knew, who I "thought" He was and who He has become to me the past few years as I've really focused on an intimate, daily connection with Him. He wants to show up in EVERY area of our lives. Do you believe that He cares about the "small things?" He does. Joyce Meyer prays over her hair, I pray over my outfits, Darrel and I pray over our investments, I pray over our appliances, our dog, our nieces and nephews and families daily. I've recently started praying over my meals and the weights and reps to do in my workouts. He wants to be the forethought in every decision we make throughout the day. We think, oh, He doesn't want to be bothered with my small requests, but He does! He created the ENTIRE WORLD and everything in it in six days and then He took a nap. It's all easy for Him, He could grant us every desire of our heart, but He's not a genie, He's GOD who loves us enough to let us fall and fail so we cry out to Him to lead.

Who Are You?

What's the one thing standing in your way of reaching your goals? Is it an outside influence or is it your own excuses or self-sabotage? I've had to have some tough conversations with myself about my actions and choices. It isn't always easy, but growth rarely is. You can't spell challenge without CHANGE, so decide what goals you have, commit to your plan, and watch how you succeed over time. This isn't a race, not even a marathon; this is a never-ending journey with bumps and turns and hills and valleys. Learn to enjoy every part of the process because when you struggle through a tough workout, when you're on the mountain top it feels great, but when you struggle through a tough workout in your valley, you prove to yourself that you really CAN do hard things.

Remember too, that if your goals don't scare you, set the bar higher. Your goals should be so unattainable you must come to the foot of the cross every day to ask God to give you the strength to push through them. Ask Him to lead and guide you as you set your schedule above. Ask Him to open the hearts and minds of your spouse or the people in your life who you need to cover you so you can give yourself that 30 minutes to sweat out your struggles. I read in *Jesus Calling* years ago, that God is in control of time. t's true; I've prayed and asked for Him to give me enough time to complete a workout so I can still make it to "this" appointment on time or that I'll have enough time to wash my hair AND make a shake. And guess what, He always provides. Ask Him for the things you think seem small, because to Him, if they're big to you, He wants to answer them.

Stop being afraid to ask hard questions of yourself, your spouse, and the people you love. We're not doing any favors to anyone by allowing ourselves to live a half-life, not fully grasping all the goodness God has to offer. He put each one of us on

~~(Un)~~ Forgiven

this Earth to make a difference. Do you really want to get to the end of your life and have Him ask you why you didn't listen or why you didn't fully trust His desire and willingness to pore over EVERY aspect of your life? I don't and I can't imagine you do either.

We Are His

Everything you own belongs to Him; your possessions, your money, your kids and clothes, are ALL gifts from God. Take care of them like they're on loan, because guess what? They are. I listened to a podcast once, I'm not even sure who it was, and he said, "Are you willing to do the work it takes to become the person you want to become?" Only you can decide. We all have the same fruits of the Spirit that God did when He hung on that cross and rose from the dead. Do you know what the fruits of the Spirit are? Peace. Love. Joy. Patience. Goodness. Gentleness. Faithfulness. Kindness. Self-Control. Hmmmm self-control…. Wait, that's a fruit of the Spirit? YES, it is…. The women in my online fit camp often tell me, "Well, I just don't have self-control." I ask them if they know Jesus (they do). "Ummm yes," they say. Well then, you have it, you need to pray over it then practice it... Are you WILLING to do the work it takes to become the woman you want to become?

Well, lean in. We've GOT to lean in. Share your truth with someone who will listen and pray over you. Talk to someone who will give you Godly advice. Far too often we take advice from people closest to us, who sometimes don't want us to succeed because it casts a shadow over their life. Be very careful who you take advice from. Not everyone, even those closest to you, is looking out for YOUR best interest. As hard as that is to admit, you KNOW you have people in your life who'd rather see you sit on the sidelines than do anything to either bring attention to yourself or God or take you away from who they "think" you should be. So, I'm going to ask you. Who are you most worried about disappointing? God and His incredible call on your life, or someone who wants to keep you small so you don't outshine them? Be careful here.

Building a network marketing (NM) business has its ups and

~~(Un)~~ Forgiven

downs, as does building any kind of business. But the hardest I've found is the people closest to you just don't understand it. And you must be okay with that fact. NM can build a significant life of freedom for anyone willing to invest their time. I've talked with SO many people who've quit or felt like they "failed" when the proper expectations weren't met. I tell people all the time if they're considering it, it's hard, but worthwhile if you're willing to get out of your comfort zone and grow. It's amazing what happens when you stay in faith and keep going. My faith, to be honest, is the ONLY thing that's gotten me this far. I *know* God has big plans for my business, I need to stay in my lane, be obedient, and watch Him work. I feel like it's two steps forward and a thousand back, but He's building and molding and shaping me along the way. What is the big dream God has placed on your heart? Hint: if it doesn't scare you or if it's something you can do on your own, it isn't big enough. Let God lead. Let Him provide the way. Pray for it. Fast over it, (we'll get to that later), but "be still" and trust; He will make it happen when the time is right. "Do not grow weary in doing good, for you will reap harvest in due time if you stay in faith and do not give up." (Galatians 6:9) This verse is the only thing that's gotten me through the last few years of my life. To God be the glory; He has done so many great things, loved the world so much that He gave us His Son. Never discount your ability to make a HUGE impact for the Kingdom, say a prayer, make a plan, step out in faith and watch how He starts to work in your life.

I'm a schedule kind of gal; I like my checklists because like a squirrel, my brain is constantly moving from one thing to the next. It's not ADD, it's just LIFE. The older I get the more I realize that I get to choose. I get to CHOOSE to set my phone away from my bed at night; I choose to get up early. I get to CHOOSE to spend my first moments with God before I pick up my phone. I get to CHOOSE to eat a whole, healthy breakfast and to exercise. I get to CHOOSE to walk to my office as I repeat my affirmations out loud and work a business that brings me joy. WE GET TO CHOOSE. What do you choose today?

As Christians, we should be CHOOSING Jesus first thing, every day. No excuses. I recently read somewhere about a woman in the 1800's who would constantly walk and talk and work and pray, she'd flail her arms in the air, she was always in communion with God. HOW COOL IS THAT?! She said, "If I only give God five minutes of my time, what if He only gives me five minutes of His blessings?" And isn't that the truth? What IF we spent as much time talking to God as we do work our business or scrolling social media or watching the newest episode of whatever on Netflix? What if… What if you replaced your scroll with your prayer life? What a glorious world this would be! I know I need to be better at this too.

The thing about God is He loves us even when we mess up, when we seem unlovable. His love is NOT conditional, just like we love our kids or fur kids or nieces and nephews, the people we would die for. He loves us MORE. You are never too far from His graces or His blessings or His love and forgiveness. Never. Ever. In Him, we are forgiven!

We've somehow built this idea in our heads about having to be perfect people, living perfect lives, with money and things and perfect bodies, and that is NOT who God calls us to be. He calls us to love and serve and make disciples. Of course, He offers blessings to some in the form of financial blessings and public profiles, but that isn't everyone. And it isn't FOR everyone. We must eliminate this perfectionism from our vocabulary and get back to the root of Jesus and His purpose for this life. Are you ready for it? Can you handle it? It's L O V E… Were you waiting for a grand answer? Well, this IS grand if we appreciate it the way it was intended. Stop putting so much pressure on yourself to be perfect. What God says is to be will be, in His time, on His schedule, and we all know it usually isn't the one we'd like.

Fruit

Have you ever experienced a miracle? Have you ever wondered how something you prayed for actually happened? Or didn't, but it worked out better? Do you believe that God wants to perform miracles in your life? I've shared with you my prayer for my future husband, that he would move in next door. Do you believe that God has a sense of humor? I do, and I have witnessed it over and over in my life, but Darrel moving in next door is by far my favorite. It was a specific prayer and God provided.

Do you believe in deliverance? Do you believe in radical healing? Do you believe in prophecy? Do you believe in angels living among you, going to work on your behalf? Have you ever witnessed a miracle? Have you ever seen something or felt something or knew something before it happened? That is the Holy Spirit prompting you, my friend. That is God intervening in your life to push you towards your purpose, towards the life He created for you.

Do you know what your spiritual gifts are? We all have them. I would encourage you to pray over them and ask God to reveal them to you if you're unsure. I used to think my gift was helping others get healthy, but it isn't. My gifts are encouragement and teaching, I get to use scripture to help my clients lean not on their understanding about health, fitness, and discipline; I get to encourage them to push into their faith.

He moves when we commune with Him, He speaks when we listen. We may not hear His audible voice as Moses did, but we have the Holy Spirit living inside of us that is our constant access to the Heavenly Father. And if you're not a believer and this all seems "hinky" to you, do the research yourself. Time after time, believer after believer, many of us have stories of divine intervention with God leading the way. Have you ever heard someone speak in tongues? It's not gibberish, it's not made up, it's the heart of God pouring out of a believer. Don't discount it just because it makes you uncomfortable. Our faith calls us to be UNCOMFORTABLE. Life should be uncomfortable. If you're comfortable in life, you're not growing. We need to be SERVING and growing as God calls us to, not what's comfortable. Have you heard the phrase, "Your comfort zone may be nice, but nothing grows there"? It is SO true! Seek out your spiritual gifts; lay your worries down at the foot of the cross. People WILL JUDGE YOU. LET THEM! You're not answering to them at the end of your life, only Christ, who hung on a cross for you. I know you want to serve for Him, I know the ache is there to obey; taking the first step is the hardest part, trust me. I have been there and am still there. Find comfort knowing that He will give you everything you need; do you believe it? Will you receive it today? Write down one thing you feel He's called you to do and start praying over it. Ask Him to give you the steps you need, the strength you need, then be willing to go!

~~(Un)~~ Forgiven

The Plan

How can we expect to pour into others if our cup is empty? Can we just talk about this for a hot minute? I see it all the time with my clients. Moms everywhere feel like it's selfish to spend 30 minutes a day exercising. Believe me when I tell you, it's not. You deserve to feel your best. You take care of everyone; spend 30 minutes on yourself. Invest in your health, MAKE time, schedule your sweat-sesh as you'd schedule your hair appointment or dentist appointment. I've never met anyone who regretted a workout, only the ones they miss. So, how can you make yourself a priority when life seems so out of control? Here are a few tips I recommend to my busy clients:

1. Get a weekly calendar and enter all your commitments, dates and times. So, if you work, you mark out your work times. My girl Mary takes all her workout stuff to work with her and exercises in her office during her lunch hour. She's taken two sets of weights to work and leaves them there and she packs her clothes for the week and leaves them and packs her lunch to make sure she stays on track with her goals. She's lost over 30 pounds in two months, so I'd say it's working. Last week her daughter wanted to be picked up early from school, but Mary said, "You'll have to wait until I'm done with my workout." That is self-love; she loves herself and her family enough to set healthy boundaries. I *love* that!

2. Enter any extra-curricular activities or dinners out, appointments, etc.
3. Factor in family time.
4. Find the empty spaces. For some of you, you need to get up earlier. Stop hitting snooze ten times; just get up the first time and you'd have your workout in. Stop rushing out the door. Wake up in plenty of time, spend time with God (note the Miracle Morning section). And get your sweat on. If mornings just don't work, then you MUST make sure you get it done in the evening. If you want to reach your goals, you must sacrifice one thing, your EXCUSES. Trust me, I have plenty of my own. I never wanted to get up at 4 a.m., but now that I do, it's become a blessing to me. I have plenty of time with hubby in the morning to do our devotionals, eat a balanced breakfast, and work out before I need to be in my home office.
5. Write down your goals daily. It will help you in those times you want to skip your appointment. DON'T do it. Write them down daily, with a 1-3 step action plan on how to achieve them.

REMEMBER that no one can take your goals or your time from you unless you allow it. Even your baby! Hold her while you exercise; build that habit for both of you. She'll love the attention and you'll get the BONUS of added weight, therefore added muscle! WIN/WIN!

You are responsible for you. Maybe you need to chat with your spouse about manning the kids while you take 30 minutes to yourself. Maybe you can get a babysitter a few days a week for an hour or so. Whatever it takes to get what YOU need, do it. You are worth the investment, and you are WORTH the time. See what scripture says about your body; you are the living tem-

~~(Un)~~ Forgiven

ple of God. The Israelites had to travel to meet God in the tabernacle; the cloud would come over the tent when He was present. When Jesus ascended to heaven, the Spirit of God came down when you confess Jesus is Lord and He lives IN you. Your body is HIS, sent to do His will. We must rest her, move her, hydrate her, and talk kindly to her. She is yours, on loan, until the day He calls you home. Love her like she's Jesus, because in a sense, she is.

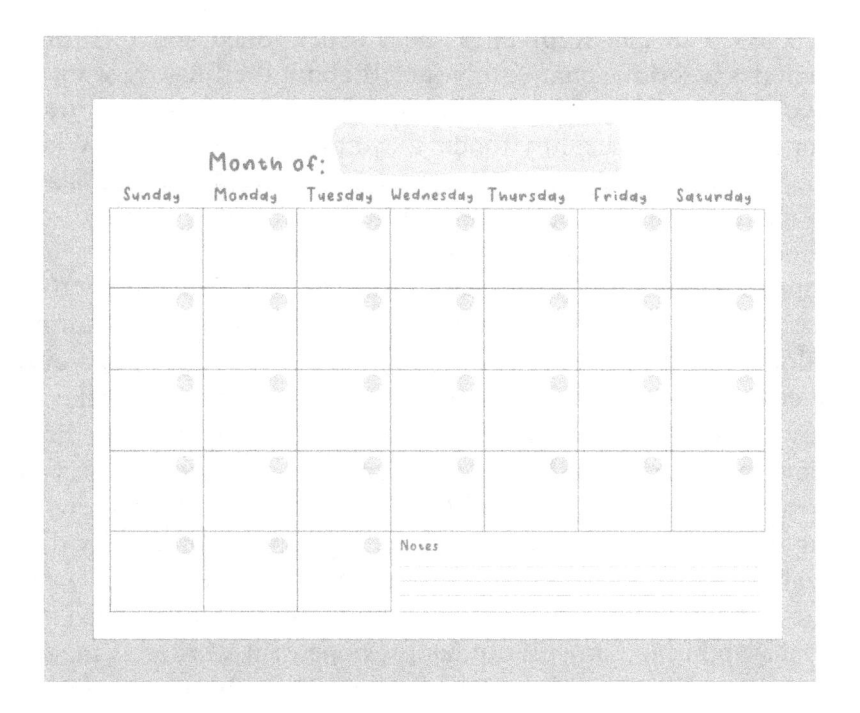

Discipline

Can we talk about honoring God with our food choices for a second? Can we talk about the things in our lives we need to work through so we can stop relying on food for comfort? It starts with that forgiveness deal I mentioned above. It also includes a serious chat with yourself about the life you want to live and the life you're willing to WORK for. When we train our bodies to eat healthy foods, they crave healthy foods. When we train them to drink water, they crave water. It takes 21 days to make or break a habit and a minimum of 66 to build discipline in a certain area of life, so I can assure you that this won't happen overnight or be an easy task. I would challenge you to ask yourself if you're putting food above God; are you putting calorie counting or your carb-eliminating diet or abs or exercise over God? We can so easily build idols in our lives that take us away from Him. I know, I do it too! The things that I share here are things I have struggled with or am now struggling with; you are not alone. I AM IN THE PIT WITH YOU! Until we are willing to say, okay Lord, my yo-yo dieting hasn't worked, my diet hasn't worked, my no carb diet hasn't worked, exercise hasn't worked, I have abs now, but I'm still not happy. I've reached my goal weight but I'm still not happy, none of it worked. I'm still not happy. When we don't heal from our inner hurts, no amount of weight loss will make you happy.

We focus so much on weight loss at the beginning of the year, but we leave God out of our goal setting. Why? Who do you think cares more about our goals than we do? Who do you think has the perfect plan for our lives? Our health? Our jobs? Who do you think cares more about our relationships than God does? Well, no one. And if you don't know Jesus, I suspect that you're curious or you probably wouldn't be reading this. Let me just say that He loves you. He loves you so completely, it's sometimes hard to understand. He died for you, knowing you may never truly know the depth of His love for you; He did it anyway, so that you just might. I suggest you get a Bible, or download the YouVersion app on your phone. It's free and there's a TON of studies you can do there that will help you understand the depth of the love He has for you.

Don't wait until a new year to set a goal and don't set a goal without first talking with God about it. Let Him lead your vision, your life, your health, your relationships. Leaving God out of it is only going to make it harder. If you give it all up to Him and let Him do the work, He's going to "make it better than you can imagine!" How do I know? (Ephesians 3:20) promises it. Don't leave Him out; let Him tell you the VISION He has for your life, let Him set the goals.

I'd take some time to write down the dreams and desires of your heart, make some weekly, monthly, quarterly goals, even yearly goals. Then pray over them, one by one, and be willing to knock off any of the ones He tells you to. Are you willing to give up something you think you want if it means God will replace it with something so much better?

You can't keep reading books that tell you what to do and not do it. I've done that. It's wasteful and unproductive. Take messy action! I like to write down my goals three months at a time, then break them down by week so they're measurable. If I have a business goal or weight loss goal or water intake goal, it's much easier to break it down backwards so I have intentional daily steps than to just wing it and hope for the best. Once you have spent intentional time in solitude with God, read your Bible verses, devotional, or daily development, take one to three things you learned from what you read that day, ask Him to guide your path, write it down and how you'll IMPLEMENT it into your day or weekly plan in one to three steps. Slow and steady is what wins.

Every morning hubs and I get up at 4 a.m. to do our devotions together, pray, and read the Bible before he leaves for work. My goal every day is to thank God for breath and life before my feet hit the floor. Not everyone woke up today; we've got to stop taking it for granted. I read *Miracle Morning* by Hal Elrod years ago and I used his methods to become a morning person, I've done a miracle morning for six years now, seven days a week. Working from home allows me a good 90 minutes to pray, read, journal, and be in the presence of God. Whatever I read or study, I make sure to ask God how I can apply it to my life today. Spending time in prayer and in God's Word is the ONLY way I start my morning; it sets the tone for my entire day. If you're just starting out, I'd say read one to three verses, pray over them, ask what He would have you take away and how can you apply it today.... Then I read a book focused on my business and how to build it for Him. Then I journal. I write down my goals, my monthly goals and long-term goals. I read *Kingdom Driven Entrepreneur* by Shae Bynes a few years ago. She helps you craft a prayer specifically for your business; I repeat this prayer daily out loud. Then I do my out loud affirmations: I AM. I am a child of the most High God. I am the head and not the tail. I will accomplish my dreams. I am a published writer; I am debt free. I am a good wife. I'm not a mother yet, but when I am I want to be the best one I can be. I am, I am, I am. What are your "I ams"? Some people think affirmations are weird, but we say things like, "I'm tired. I'm fat. I'm not motivated" and what happens? You BECOME those things. So why not say the things you HOPE to be so you can step into those instead of the lies of the enemy? Let go of the control you think you need to have over your life and let Him in. He will work WONDERS for your present and your future, but you've got to let Him in and do what He desires to do.

Trust

 Want the job? Pray over it and go! Want the guy? Pray over it and ask him out! Want a raise? Pray over it and ask! Want to build a business or start a healthy journey?! Pray over it, ask His blessings, and GO! You KNOW that dream you have is there for a reason. Do you believe God has your best interest at heart? Do you trust where He leads? Are you willing to step out in faith even if it means you struggle and fall? Do you trust that He will give you what you need?

 I love you enough to tell you that you need to get up and fight for it. The world needs you to live in your purpose, beloved. The devil loves it when we're distracted, when we procrastinate, when we doubt. There is hurt in the world, there are sick kids, homeless veterans, abused animals, lonely elderly people…. So many causes out there that can keep us up at night. What's yours? I read a LOT of personal development, every day I start with prayer, reading a faith-based book focused on business, and my Bible. That ache in your soul to speak to women isn't there by chance, He's put that ache there and wants you to seek His will for what it can become. That ache to adopt or help veterans or the elderly, it's there for a reason. We are called to love people and make disciples. How can we honor Him with our work today? How can we step into faith and believe that He will provide all we need? It's okay to have a desire to build a successful business if you're in it to give glory to God and serve others. We were never called to live paycheck to paycheck; we're called to take care of the widows and orphans. Even Jesus, during His ministry, was staying in the best places, wearing the nice clothes and sandals of that time. Everywhere you go, you are a representation of Jesus Christ. So, no more wearing your pjs to Wal-Mart or driving a dirty car or living in an unclean home. The Great Commission tells us to share God's Word and make disciples;

Lindy Schlabach

we get to share Him with everyone we meet. Sometimes it's through our words, our story, other times it's through a first impression. People are more responsive to learning from someone who represents Jesus as He intended, and that means using and taking care of our gifts. When we host people in our homes, it is our opportunity to glorify Him; when we're out in public, the same rings true. Everything we have is on loan from Him and He's blessed us with it so we can use it to serve others. How are you representing Him with your gifts today?

Boundaries

What or who is holding you back from living God's best for your life? Usually, it's someone close to us that we need to set a boundary with. Sometimes it's a spouse or parent or kid or best friend. Maybe it's a grandparent or co-worker or sibling. We love our families SO much and we want the best for them, of course! But often that comes with not respecting boundaries. I know that for my own family, this is a HUGE issue. We've been breaking boundaries my whole life! So much so that when my cousin shared her revelation with me about a month ago, I said, "YESSSSS! You are SO RIGHT!"

But how do we change it now? Well, it's never too late. And we do it with love; love is ALWAYS the answer. Sometimes a simple conversation will suffice. If it's someone who loves you, they're usually grateful for the observation and are willing to respect the boundaries you put in place. How do you do that with someone you live with or a child who doesn't understand the word? With kids, it's a bit different, but I think all kids should learn the benefit of boundaries, so they're not taken advantage of or manipulated as they grow up. What a concept! Of course, our spouses will be the hardest, but they love you most! They committed to a life with you; setting boundaries is VITAL for a happy marriage.

You can set time boundaries, physical boundaries, conversational boundaries, relationship boundaries, personal boundaries, and content boundaries. I love ALL these ideas. Let's break them down a bit.

Time Boundaries- I had to learn to set a time boundary with my business. I answer messages and check social media at specific times of the day. This took YEARS. I think if we all did this as it relates to scrolling our feeds, we'd have a lot more time in the day to do all the things we need to do.

Physical Boundaries- these are especially good for our kids to learn. What is and is not appropriate for your personal space? Set it, live it, and don't make anyone feel guilty about it. If your kid doesn't want to hold hands or hug someone, don't make them. They're allowed to have their own boundaries.

Conversational Boundaries- topics you are and are not open to discussing. Maybe it's politics (this one rarely ends well if you're on opposing sides), but how about gossip? We know what scripture says about it: it's a sin and to even participate in it is sin. Is that a boundary you need to set?

Relationship Boundaries- these are usually mutually agreed upon between your partner and close friends and family. Maybe you don't mind if they "pop in," maybe you do. Set clear boundaries with your people.

Personal Boundaries- don't apologize for these and don't shame someone for theirs. They may have experienced some sort of trauma you're unaware of. Always respect other people's boundaries. These can be boundaries within yourself, too, that you know keep you from going back to old ways or ensuring you're staying on track with God's way and not the world's way.

And lastly, one of my favorites but one we don't talk about a lot.

Content Boundaries- Listen up, Christians! Things you will or will not consume as it relates to the type of television you watch, the music you listen to, what reels you watch on social media, and the language of the songs you listen to is so important! This is a big one for me. If there are too many curse words in the first three minutes of a movie, I'm out. I don't have time for inappropriate use of my God's name or a certain "F" bomb that many movies think just must be in there. We reap what we sow, we put out what we put in; that goes for food, movement, movies, music, and relationships. If you crave intimacy with God, remove the junk in your life.

Set boundaries for yourself. Respect the ones others set for themselves and let your kids set their own. They know who and

~~(Un)~~ Forgiven

what they're comfortable with. You've raised them right; let them decide who gets in their personal space.

Spiritual Discipline

Let's talk about fasting for a second. Do you fast? Do you know what the Bible says about fasting? It's not a "do if you wish" act; it's commanded by God. He says, "when you fast." For years I felt called to fast, but I didn't know what I was doing or how I was to do it. Then in all God fashion, our pastor preached a message on it. Here's how he explained it, referencing Luke 18, Luke 4, Matthew 6, and Zachariah.

1. When you fast, be aware of your fallen nature, your sin and God's holiness. If you think "I'm hungry" then you're not fulfilled with God. Realize your sin and in those moments of extreme hunger, pray over them, for Him to break your chains.

2. Break your chains. Push INTO the fast. Become more like Him. Every time I fast, I'm aware of a certain sin in my life, so in those moments of extreme hunger, I pray over that sin, that He would take it from me. Sometimes it's something major. The last fast I did, He broke my chains to Club crackers. It sounds so silly, doesn't it? But anything that takes our eyes off Jesus first is a chain that needs broken.

3. Expectation of change. Empathy. Feel the feelings of others. Fast for our country, our government, our teachers and medical professionals, our military men and

women, your lost family, broken relationships, finances. Anything! All of it! FAST! Let Him break your chains.

I've never felt closer to God than when I fast. Some people do a 24 hour fast; my goal is always three days, but 42 hours is the longest I've gone but I always could've gone longer. Lean on Him to sustain you.

If you truly want to connect with God in a new and deeper way, fast. Pray over your fast, when to do it, how long to do it. But do it, don't make excuses. You'll be amazed at how GOOD and connected you feel.

Prayer

How do you DO the thing you're called to do when you have no idea how to do it?! Well, prayer. You're going to find the common theme throughout this book is prayer. It IS the MOST powerful WEAPON we have. Prayer is a direct connection to God through the Holy Spirit living inside you. We must pray against the enemy, and prayer is a gift we so often take for granted. If you're a believer and have asked God into your heart, you have the Holy Spirit living within you, which is a direct LINE to God! How COOL is that?! My goodness, that should get our hearts PUMPING for Jesus and prayer through the entire day! He will lead and guide us in EVERY decision we make, from what to wear to what to eat, how to move, love, talk, work, be a mom or wife or husband. He wants to be involved in every seemingly small detail of your life. If you have yet to find your purpose in life, yet you KNOW you're called for more, seek His will, seek His face, come to Him through prayer and supplication and let Him outline a plan for you. He will. He did for me with this book; He will for you too. Before Genesis 1, He had a plan for you. He knew everything about you, how you'd look, your strengths and weaknesses, your struggles and your triumphs. He thought you worthy enough to be born, so don't let Him down. You have a divine calling on your life, and if you're willing to lean in, get uncomfortable for God and step into His plans for you, He will provide the outline.

We're so worried about WHO we'll be by 25-30, we forget that most people who've made ANY kind of impact in this world were older, mid-late 30's in some cases, but usually 40+. Think of Jesus; His ministry didn't begin until he was 30 and ended at 33. I am in my 40's and I'm telling you, I've never felt so encouraged, so motivated and determined to live God's best for my life. I almost threw in the towel, which is JUST what the devil wants, but my MISSION is bigger than myself. My passion is bigger than any setback or frustration could ever be. God is in control of my LIFE, my relationship, my marriage, my income, my everything. Everything I have is His. Everything you have is a blessing from Him. Don't sell your dream and your conviction short because you're afraid to fail. I'm going to promise you that you're going to fail. But John C. Maxwell calls it "Failing Forward." We don't fail and fall; we fail, learn, and move forward. THAT is what it means to fail forward. Don't be afraid to struggle with something new, but be TERRIFIED to not live out God's plan for your life and face Him at the end having not done all He called you to. That teeny, tiny little voice in your head that doesn't seem to quiet down, that's the Holy Spirit calling you, my love. So, GO, and let God do a mighty work in your life.

In what areas of life do you hold shame? There is probably at least one. I know I have a few. We are a constant work in progress; owning your shame takes courage. Shame is a tactic the enemy uses to keep us procrastinating what God has called us to. How can we prayerfully address any shame you're holding onto?

How can we let it go? It is a daily, sometimes moment by moment battle but you've got to pray for strength and ask God to reveal the areas of shame you're holding on to, many of which you may be unaware of. We can hold shame in our physical appearance, our sexual past, our food choices, our vanity, an affair or lust after another human being. We can hold shame for an abortion or disordered eating. We can hold shame for spending money we shouldn't... the list goes on and on. When Jesus took His last breath on that cross, what did He say? He said, IT IS FINISHED (emphasis added). IT. IS. FINISHED (John 19:30). My friends, we've got to lay our burdens at the cross. Sometimes we can let it go once and other times we must let it go over and over again. But first you must acknowledge that it even exists and be willing to confront it, bless it, and release it from your life. We are all just trying to live the best we can.

You are NOT alone. We MUST start to talk about some of these things, because if we don't the devil is right there ready to fill your head with lies that will never serve you and quite honestly, it's keeping you from living God's best for your life. Is that really what you want? To be shirking about judging yourself so harshly that you're never able to see the amazing, beautiful, incredible human you are? I don't think anyone wants that. I think we just live so paralyzed by it we don't know where to even begin.

I want you to think about the shameful parts of your life. Write them down. Then, one by one ask God to take them from you. Guess what, He will. THEN LET IT GO. That's the hard part, because life happens between our ears and it's our own condemnation that keeps us from living God's best. So, over and over you have to give it over to God and ask God to heal your heart and your head. You CAN be free from food addiction, from disordered eating, from lust and gluttony and debt and sexual immorality. The devil loves it when we hold on to it and he uses it to shame us, but sometimes it's our own thoughts that are the ones that keep coming back; I know mine do.

I just look up if I'm in a crowd. Or I take a deep breath with my eyes closed. He KNOWS your heart. He will take it from you, but stop picking it up. When you ask Him to forgive you, BAM! He does; your slate is WIPED CLEAN! So why do we keep picking it up? Letting go takes PRACTICE; depending on your shame-scale it could take years. But it IS a discipline you can continue to practice, repeatedly, until you're free. Keep looking up; just say "Jesus" and see how the peace that passes all understanding wipes away the noise.

Be Encouraged!

There is NOTHING that He doesn't know about you. There isn't anything that will keep Him from loving you. Dig up those seeds that are holding you back. He already knows. He will never shame you. If the thoughts in your head are encouraging and loving and moving you towards positive change, THAT is the Holy Spirit's prompting. If what you hear is negative or shaming, that is evil and you need to, in that moment, REBUKE those thoughts in Jesus's name. Father, clear my head of any thoughts that aren't of You. Let me feel the conviction through the Holy Spirit to live today as You would have me live. Remind me who Your Word says I am. In Jesus' name, amen. (Psalm 139:23-24) "Search me, God, and know my heart, test me and know my anxious thoughts. See if there is any offensive way in me and lead me in the way everlasting." This is my prayer for you.

As we begin the devotional section, I would like to encourage you to dig deep, to pray fervently, and be open to what the Holy Spirit will do through you. Leaning into God's plan for your life can often be hard, but I hope you will lean into each day as we move forward and truly connect with God and all He wants to do in your life. We get one shot, that's it. Every day is an extreme opportunity to lean into your faith and let the light of Jesus shine through you. We're chasing a deep, personal, intimate relationship with the Father, and I hope you will read and re-read this devotional as it will hopefully speak to you differently through each phase of your life. Be open, be honest, be real. While digging up past seeds of hurt is hard in the moment, the pain is temporary, but the healing is forever.

Devotionals

DAY 1

Story: I was single at 36, living in a small town with an even smaller dating pool, and I just kept praying that God would move my future husband in next door. I'd done the online dating thing, I was recovering from my surgery, feeling lost and unlovable. My surgery was in February of 2020 and later that month, my future husband would move in, you guessed it, NEXT DOOR!

Verse: Mark 11:23

"I tell you the truth, if anyone says to this mountain, go throw yourself into the sea and does not doubt in his heart but believes that what he says will happen, it will be done for him."

Scripture Application: Read the verse in its context. How will you apply the message of this verse to your life today?

_____

_____

Gratitude:

_____

_____

_____

_____

~~(Un)~~ Forgiven

Affirmations: I AM HEALTHY. I ENJOY MOVEMENT. I AM FORGIVEN.

I AM (fill in your blank)

_____

Prayer: Heavenly Father, forgive me for doubting your willingness to answer specific and big prayers. Let me pray BOLDLY today and every day. In Jesus' name, amen.

Thoughts/Notes/Encouragement/Inspiration:

_____

_____

_____

_____

DAY 2

Story: Shame. It's a common theme in my life and in the lives of many women I work with. Shame is a lie from the enemy meant to keep us bound in our sin. As a recovered emotional eater/binge eater, I can tell you how the enemy often uses food to shame me. Do you hear the lies too? Learning God's truth about who He says we are is so freeing. Let Him lead your healthy journey. You are not your past; you are who you CHOOSE to be today, ruled by the peace of Christ in your life and not the tastebuds that tell you that you '"crave" or the enemy who calls you unworthy. You are an overcomer, you are free, you are forgiven. We are new creations in Christ, He made us in His image, taken from the rib of Adam, sent to love people and make disciples! Repeat after me, I am who HE says I am!

Verse: Psalm 139:14

"I praise you because I am fearfully and wonderfully made, your works are wonderful, I know that full well."

Scripture Application: Read the verse in its context. How will you apply the message of this verse to your life today?

_____

_____

_____

Gratitude:

_____

_____

_____

~~(Un)~~ Forgiven

Affirmations: I AM FEARFULLY AND WONDERFULLY MADE. I AM A NEW CREATION IN CHRIST.

I AM (fill in your blank)

_____

Prayer: Heavenly Father, thank You for making me, me. I know I am too hard on myself sometimes, Lord, and I repent for my self-loathing and self-sabotage, in food, shopping, over-exercise, alcohol, comparison and any other area of struggle I face. Lord, I want to see me as You do, a wonderful work, intentionally created for Your good purpose. Let me live my life for You today and every day. In Jesus' name, amen.

Thoughts/Notes/Encouragement/Inspiration:

_____

_____

_____

_____

DAY 3

Story: I'm exhausted. I feel like I'm failing at everything. I was in the ER last night, my income has dipped this month, I'm not providing for my family like I had been, my body is struggling, and I feel lost and like a big disappointment. This morning, I was mid workout and a song came on by Elevation Worship. To be honest, I can't even remember which one it was, but in that moment, I felt the Holy Spirit so completely. He reminded me that I am never a disappointment, that He sees me, He is with me, and He will never leave me nor forsake me and no matter how heavy life feels, He will always be there to lessen my burden if I hand it up to Him. What an incredible blessing. We can never let God down, He sees us in our mess, He understands our anger and frustration. In our messiest times, we can bring Him our heavy load and hand it over. He will carry it for us, and the best part is that He will bring good that glorifies Him through it! Hang on, stay in faith and in prayer, let Him take your burdens; you were never meant to carry them anyway.

Verse: Matthew 11:28

"Come to me all you who are weary and burdened, and I will give you rest."

Scripture Application: *Read the verse in its context. How will you apply the message of this verse to your life today?*

_____

_____

_____

_____

~~(Un)~~ Forgiven

Gratitude:

_____

_____

_____

Affirmations: I AM FREE. I AM THE HEAD AND NOT THE TAIL. I AM FORGIVEN.

I AM (fill in your blank)

_____

Prayer: Heavenly Father, I am tired. I feel like nothing I ever do is enough. I don't know what I'm supposed to be doing. I feel like I'm letting everyone down and I need help. Please remind me who I am in You, Lord. In Jesus' name, amen.

Thoughts/Notes/Encouragement/Inspiration:

_____

_____

_____

DAY 4

Story: Think about your pit. Think about that moment when you decided that you couldn't bear one second more on your own. Do you remember it? God has brought me out of many pits; my rape, losing my grandpa and the anxiety, depression, and weight gain that it brought, my partying phase, my infertility journey, my brother getting shot, getting laid off. So many pits, some before I came back to Him, some after. He was always there, even when I didn't realize it. He was there for me, and He is there for you. I know for me, so many times I've laid my burdens at the foot of the cross only to pick them up again. But I urge you to give it to Him and let Him handle it. Our tendency in our flesh is to worry. We've already talked about how the devil loves that, but we're not playing his game. God has already won; the devil has lost, and his schemes are an attempt to be a poor sport. I won't let him win the battle in my mind, and my prayer is that you won't either. What do you need to lay down today for the LAST time? Use the lines below to write them out and ask God to remove them for you today.

Verse: Psalm 40:1-2

"I waited patiently for the Lord, He turned to me and heard my cry. He lifted me out of the pit, out of the mud and mire, He set my feet on a rock and gave me a firm place to stand."

Scripture Application: Read the verse in its context. How will you apply the message of this verse to your life today?

_____

_____

_____

~~(Un)~~ Forgiven

Gratitude:

_____

_____

Affirmations: I AM HOLY. I AM KIND. I AM HOPEFUL. I AM (fill in your blank)

_____

Prayer: Heavenly Father, You are my Rock, my firm foundation, it is on You alone that I stand. You heard me, Father, You lifted me up when I didn't see anywhere to go but down. You are the constant in my life; when everything around me feels off, You are my strong fortress. In Jesus' name, amen.

Thoughts/Notes/Encouragement/Inspiration:

_____

_____

_____

_____

DAY 5

Story: Read the verse below and let it sink in. BEFORE the creation of the world. He KNEW YOU, before the creation of the world! We say the most awful things to ourselves sometimes and I think it breaks God's heart. He loves us so much, before Genesis 1 He knew us. Can you imagine how it breaks His heart when we live in shame and self-sabotage? I gained 100 pounds after my grandpa died. Food was my BandAid. I lay on the couch in a pile of depression and the reality of his death sunk in like an anchor in the ocean. For 15 years I partied my life away, binge-drinking and eating, sleeping around, getting high. I was desperate for comfort, and it never came. One simple invitation to church in 2016 changed my life. It was a church I was hurt by as a kid, and walking in there to hear a new pastor and a new message, I didn't have a lot of hope, but I was desperate. I craved something to fill the God-shaped hole in my life. Sunday after Sunday, I couldn't wait to go back. He found me in my pit, He reignited my soul, He found me, He forgave me. While I still stumble daily, I know right where to go to mend, not in a bottle or a snack, but in the loving arms of my Heavenly Father who knew me all along. He never left me, He didn't find me, He was always there, just waiting for me to come home. Thank You, Jesus for Your unconditional love and mercy; I am a walking testament to Your grace. I love You with everything that I am.

Verse: Ephesians 1:4

"For He chose us in Him before the creation of the world to be holy and blameless in His sight."

~~(Un)~~ Forgiven

Scripture Application: Read the verse in its context. How will you apply the message of this verse to your life today?

_____

_____

Gratitude:

_____

_____

Affirmations: I AM CHOSEN. I AM (fill in your blank)

_____

Prayer: Heavenly Father, thank You for choosing me and finding me worthy. I know I'm hard on myself sometimes, Lord, and I want to offer myself the grace I so freely offer to others. You chose us all; each and every person in the world, You chose us. I want to love all Your children, Father; let me see people as You see them. You created everything in this glorious world and still You chose me. Help me love myself and see myself as holy and blameless, Lord, and help me share that gift with everyone I meet. In Jesus' name, amen.

Thoughts/Notes/Encouragement/Inspiration:

_____

_____

_____

DAY 6

Story: Oof! Our pastor shared this recently. There is God's path and your path, and hopefully yours will align with His. I like to think there are three: mine, God's, and the world's. I don't want to operate on the world's path, but I also know that while my path may partially align with God's, I often go off on my own, even if unintentionally at times. My goal is to always have my path align with His. I don't want to live for the world, and I don't want to live for myself. I pray that is the case for you. We cannot live God's path and our path; we can only choose one. How can you step off your path today and onto His? What areas are you holding on to that you know He's calling you to give up? Diet culture? Money? A relationship? You can't live both ways. Are you willing to give up your way for His?

Verse: Acts 5:29
"We must obey God rather than man."

Scripture Application: Read the verse in its context. How will you apply the message of this verse to your life today?

_____

_____

_____

Gratitude:

_____

_____

_____

_____

~~(Un)~~ Forgiven

Affirmations: I AM (fill in your blank)

_____

Prayer: Heavenly Father, You are the Way, the Truth and the Life and I want to only live for you. My flesh says I need certain things in my life, Lord, but I know that isn't the case. Seach my heart, Lord, and reveal any shred of hurt or unforgiveness or flesh that isn't in line with Your path. I am ready for true change, even if it hurts. In Jesus' name, amen.

Thoughts/Notes/Encouragement/Inspiration:

_____

_____

_____

_____

DAY 7

Story: Nothing you have is by chance. Your pantry is full because of God's provision, your car and home and clothes and kids are all to be used to glorify the Kingdom. God gave you purpose through your work or education or family so that you would receive what you need to further His Kingdom. Everything we have is to be praised because of His provision. Yes, you do the work, but He gives you the work ethic and drive. Yes, you take care of your home, because He gave you the inspiration to do so. Why are some people blessed who aren't believers? God gave them their gifts too; He's hoping they'll give glory to Him through them. Oftentimes, however, that isn't the case. We will all account for our sins; I don't want to face Him one day and have Him ask why I didn't use my blessings to honor Him. What would you have today if you woke up with only what you thanked Him for yesterday? That should call us ALL to praise Him, all day, every day.

Verse: 1 Timothy 4:4

"For everything God created is good and nothing is to be rejected if it is received with Thanksgiving."

Scripture Application: Read the verse in its context. How will you apply the message of this verse to your life today?

_____

_____

_____

_____

~~(Un)~~ Forgiven

Gratitude:

_____

_____

Affirmations: I AM (fill in your blank)

_____

Prayer: Heavenly Father, You have blessed me more than I deserve; You have blessed me more than I could imagine. The simple fact that You woke me up today is a gift, even when I'm struggling. I know not everyone received that gift today, Lord, and I don't want to take it for granted. I know sometimes I am ungrateful, and I am sorry. Thank You for my life, my family, my provision, my body. I've heard it asked that, if I woke up with only what I thanked God for yesterday, what would I have? I never want to go a day without praising You, Lord; remind me in my weakness of all You've done and will do. In Jesus' name, amen.

Thoughts/Notes/Encouragement/Inspiration:

_____

_____

_____

_____

DAY 8

Story: For years, I pushed to make life happen my way, my business, relationships, my body, and weight, instead of trusting God's plan and His timing. When we read in Isaiah, we see what happens when we let God lead. Are you prepared to wait if He calls you to, to build your mighty nation?

Verse Isaiah 60:22

"The smallest family will become 1,000 people and the tiniest group, a mighty nation. At the right time, I the Lord, will make it happen."

Scripture Application: Read the verse in its context. How will you apply the message of this verse to your life today?

_____

_____

Gratitude:

_____

_____

Affirmations: I AM WORTHY. I AM REDEEMED. I AM FORGIVEN. I AM (fill in your blank)

_____

_____

~~(Un)~~ Forgiven

Prayer: Heavenly Father, thank You for making me a mighty nation! Thank You for giving me what I need to live for You today and let me trust in Your perfect timing. In Jesus' name, amen.

Thoughts/Notes/Encouragement/Inspiration:

_____

_____

_____

_____

DAY 9

Story: I've often heard people say that you shouldn't pray for patience, because God will test you in uncomfortable ways. As a believer, however, you have patience already because you have Jesus, and patience is a fruit of the Spirit. Sometimes we must cultivate it. This is not my strong suit. What are the areas of your life where you exercise complete patience? What are the areas of your life where you could use improvement? One of the best lessons I've learned this year, through much prayer, is patience in marriage. My husband is an amazing man of God and we live very well together, even though we didn't get married until I was 40 and he was 37. After living on our own for so long, then moving in together, a certain amount of patience was necessary for us both. Marriage is our way to honor God, and while we may have times where we lose patience with each other, God reminds us how patient He has been with us in our struggles, and it makes it a whole lot easier to offer the same to each other. Who do you need to exercise more patience with?

Verse: Galatians 5:22-23

"But the fruit of the spirit is love, joy, peace, patience, kindness, gentleness, faithfulness, goodness, and self-control. Against such things there is no law."

Scripture Application: Read the verse in its context. How will you apply the message of this verse to your life today?

___

___

___

___

~~(Un)~~ Forgiven

Gratitude:

_____

_____

Affirmations: I AM JOYFUL. I AM PATIENT. I AM KIND. I AM (fill in your blank)

_____

Prayer: Heavenly Father, THANK YOU! for the fruits, thank You that I *get* to share the goodness of your fruits with others. Let me cultivate these fruits in a way that brings honor and glory to You, Lord, in all areas, around all people in my life. In Jesus' name, amen.

Thoughts/Notes/Encouragement/Inspiration

_____

_____

_____

_____

DAY 10

Story: Do you know the story of Job? Job was a faithful servant of God; the devil chose him to test his faith and God allowed it. The devil took everything from Job: his home, his living, his family, all his children, every person he ever loved. Yet Job remained faithful. Do you have faith like Job? I know I struggle here, if I'm being honest. God lovingly corrects us as a parent corrects a child, He convicts us through the Holy Spirit and invites us to redirect our paths to Him. Job had done nothing wrong, and God still allowed his life to be shaken to the core. Job remained faithful. Life comes easy to us these days; we have instant access to all things in real time. This was not the case in Job's day, and this was not the case when I grew up in the late 80's and early 90's; we went out to eat, we went to the store, life was simpler then. Life is too easy today, and I think we take much of it for granted. We groan at the slightest inconvenience or slow person on the road or in line in front of us. Compassion for each other is gone, and it shows in our lack of patience. I hope we can all learn to slow down a bit and accept the loving discipline of God when He calls us. How can we live like Job today?

Verse: Job 5:17
"Blessed is the man whom God corrects; so, do not despise the discipline of the Almighty."

Scripture Application: Read the verse in its context. How will you apply the message of this verse to your life today?

_____

_____

_____

_____

~~(Un)~~ Forgiven

Gratitude:

_____

_____

Affirmations: I AM FREE. I AM HEALED. I AM (fill in your blank)

_____

_____

Prayer: Heavenly Father, thank You for your loving correction, thank You for loving me enough to discipline me. I know that you have a calling on my life; I know that you want the most for me. Let me see your correction as love, the same way a parent corrects a child. I am Yours. In Jesus' name, amen.

Thoughts/Notes/Encouragement/Inspiration:

_____

_____

_____

_____

_____

DAY 11

Story: The verse below has been my prayer for the past few months; it comes to mind almost daily. Change me, Lord. Unsettle me, break me, tear me apart from the top down and inside out. Shred everything of my flesh that isn't of You. I want to be so Holy Spirit-led I can't even remember my flesh. Do you ache for that kind of connection? I hope so; it's what changes the world. Never stop stepping out in courage, never get comfortable with where you are in life, always be pushing toward growth, leaning into scripture, and letting Him change you in the best way. When we seek true Holy Spirit connection, we see the hand of God in everything we do. I want that kind of life; I want that kind of obedience. I'm exhausted from trying it my way, aren't you? Will you use this verse as your prayer and let Him reveal your weak spots so He can create in you a new heart and a new level of obedience?

Verse: Psalm 139:23-24
"Search me God and know my heart, test me, and know my anxious thoughts. See if there is any offensive way in me and lead me in the way everlasting."

Scripture Application: Read the verse in its context. How will you apply the message of this verse to your life today?

_____

_____

_____

_____

_____

~~(Un)~~ Forgiven

Gratitude:

_____

_____

Affirmations: I AM (fill in your blank)

_____

_____

Prayer: Heavenly Father, break me apart, unsettle me, change me, reveal to me the weak spots I've buried deep and let my flesh cry out to You for a new way. I don't want to live outside of Your will; I want to step fully into the life of obedience You've called me to. Search me, Lord, and know my heart, test me, and know my anxious thoughts. See if there is any offensive way in me and lead me in the way everlasting. In Jesus' name, amen.

Thoughts/Notes/Encouragement/Inspiration:

_____

_____

_____

_____

DAY 12

Story: Do you trust God? Like, actually trust Him? We say we do, but sometimes our actions say otherwise. How can we, in moments of panic or fear, lean into prayer and let His Word soothe our aching spirits? Another fruit of the spirit is peace; we must seek His perfect peace at all costs. Of course, we trust Him, we KNOW His plans are better, we've experienced it, in good times and bad. This verse is the perfect reminder of His steadfast love and His promise to always provide what we need. Your only hope is in Jesus; remember during times of chaos that looking up, saying His name, closing your eyes even if you're in public and it feels weird, He will comfort you. He is our rock, He is our Redeemer, we trust in His steadfast love. We will all have times of worry or doubt, we're human, but in the next second, in the next choice we can repent and ask Him to remind us again. He is a patient God; aren't we thankful for that today?

Verse: Isaiah 26:3

"You will keep in perfect peace him whose mind is steadfast because He trusts in you."

Scripture Application: Read the verse in its context. How will you apply the message of this verse to your life today?

_____

_____

Gratitude:

_____

_____

_____

~~(Un)~~ Forgiven

Affirmations: I AM TRUSTING. I AM ABLE. I AM (fill in your blank)

_____

_____

Prayer: Heavenly Father, my worry gets to me sometimes. The spirit is willing, but my flesh is weak. I'm thankful that You know my weak spots and are always quick to remind me of Your peace and Your presence. I come to You with all I have, Lord, let me feel peace in my chaos today. In Jesus' name, amen.

Thoughts/Notes/Encouragement/Inspiration:

_____

_____

_____

_____

DAY 13

Story: I started hemorrhaging in September of 2018, the worst year of my life. My brother got shot, I got laid off, I couldn't sink any lower, or could I…debt from my inability to work, constant visits to the ER, medical menopause, I couldn't leave the house without packing clothes, among other things. After countless surgeries, the doctor said a hysterectomy was necessary. I was devastated.

Verse: John 16:33
"I have told you these things so that in me you may have peace. In this world you *will* have trouble, but take heart, I have overcome the world." (emphasis added)

Scripture Application: Read the verse in its context. How will you apply the message of this verse to your life today?

_____

_____

Gratitude:

_____

_____

Affirmations: I AM DETERMINED. I AM FOCUSED. I AM A PERSON OF ACTION.

I AM (fill in your blank)

_____

_____

_____

~~(Un)~~ Forgiven

Prayer: Heavenly Father, life is hard. My circumstances seem out of control and not at all what I'd hoped, but I know You work my struggle out for Your glory. Lead me, Lord, to Your truth today and every day; thank You for continued peace. In Jesus' name, amen.

Thoughts/Notes/Encouragement/Inspiration:

_____

_____

_____

_____

_____

DAY 14

Story: God calls us in Proverbs to lean NOT on our own understanding. That is a tall order at times, isn't it? When I was recovering from my hysterectomy, I was feeling broken and ashamed, unlovable, and unworthy. I didn't understand why I had to go through what I did. I had always dreamt of being pregnant. Who would want me now?

Verse Proverbs 3: 5-6

"Trust in the Lord with all your heart and lean not on your own understanding. In all your ways acknowledge him and he will make your path straight."

Scripture Application: Read the verse in its context. How will you apply the message of this verse to your life today?

_____

_____

Gratitude:

_____

_____

Affirmations: I AM CHOSEN. I AM GRATEFUL. I AM FORGIVEN. I AM (fill in your blank)

_____

_____

_____

~~(Un)~~ Forgiven

Prayer: Heavenly Father, I don't always understand what You're doing, but I'm grateful I don't have to. Thank You for always having my best in mind. In Jesus' name, amen.

Thoughts/Notes/Encouragement/Inspiration:

_____

_____

_____

_____

_____

DAY 15

Story: It's easy to get wrapped up in politics or the latest trends, but what does it all mean? Why does it all matter? Does it matter? When God is the Lord of our lives, His path is the one we seek, not the shallow offerings of the world that can never fill us. Our pastor said last week that there are two paths, your path and God's path. We hope that our path becomes God's path, but it can't be the world's path. We see the unveiling of scripture before our eyes, and many people will say these are "end times." But truly we don't know, and instead of wishing for the return of Christ, let us make disciples and share with the lost. We have to live in the world, but we don't have to live for the world. Sometimes I don't know what to think or feel about the things I see or hear that are happening in the world, but I do know that my comfort comes from knowing God has already won. If you find yourself being overwhelmed by the latest headlines, redirect your thoughts. Turn off the news and let's focus on what we do know, that God isn't surprised by what's happening, and He will use it all for His good at the right time. Will you trust in that today?

Verse: 1 John 2:15-17
"Do not love the world or anything in the world. If anyone loves the world, the love of the Father is not in him. For everything in the world, the lust of the flesh, the lust of the eyes and the pride of life comes not from the Father but from the world. The world and its desires pass away but those who do the will of God live forever."

Scripture Application: Read the verse in its context. How will you apply the message of this verse to your life today?

_____

_____

_____

~~(Un)~~ Forgiven

Gratitude:

_____

_____

Affirmations: I AM HEALTHY. I AM ACTIVE. I AM GOOD. I AM LIGHT!

I AM (fill in your blank)

_____

Prayer: Heavenly Father, the world is in turmoil and offers many things that I know aren't of You. Help me to focus on Your path, Lord; I want to live for You alone. Help me to be a light in the darkness and let Your light shine so brightly that the world will ask why I am the way that I am. I can't wait to give glory to You in everything I do. Lord, let me start with every second of every day. In Jesus' name, amen.

Thoughts/Notes/Encouragement/Inspiration:

_____

_____

_____

_____

DAY 16

Story: In 2018 I got laid off, my brother got shot (he survived), and I started hemorrhaging, I believe from all the stress of the year, then started my infertility journey which eventually led to a hysterectomy. It was two years of trials, one after the other, but I stayed in faith. Through that time, my business grew, my dad got sober, and two months after my surgery, I met my now husband. When it all began, I didn't see a way, but I'd been back in church for 18 months and was determined not to be beaten by my circumstances but to give God my all. He more than provided. He brought blessing after blessing through my struggles. Scripture promises trials, but also that "God has already overcome." (John 16:33) We may not always feel the joy, but we must at least "consider it." (James 1:2) Whatever struggle you find yourself facing today, know that God sees you and He hurts with you. You are not alone.

Verse: James 1:2

"Consider is pure joy, brothers and sisters when you face trials of many kinds, because the testing of your faith produces perseverance."

Scripture Application: Read the verse in its context. How will you apply the message of this verse to your life today?

_____

_____

_____

_____

_____

~~(Un)~~ Forgiven

Gratitude:

_____

_____

Affirmation*s*: I AM JOYFUL. I AM GRATEFUL. I AM ANNOINTED.

I AM (fill in your blank)

_____

Prayer: Heavenly Father, I struggle to find joy in the chaos, but I know Your Word tells me to. Help me to remember every second of the day that You are FOR me and that I am never alone, that in my darkest days You are there for me. Let me glorify You in my struggles today, Lord, and while I may not understand, my faith tells me I don't have to. In Jesus' name, amen.

Thoughts/Notes/Encouragement/Inspiration:

_____

_____

_____

_____

DAY 17

Story: What are you afraid of? What makes you anxious? How can you, in those moments, remember to look up, or say His name? Fear is a liar, sent straight from the pit of hell. The Bible tells us over and over "do not fear," yet we do. As believers, I think fear is one of the biggest tactics of the enemy. We KNOW our Sovereign God is in control, yet a feeling of fear comes, and it takes us over completely. I waited a long time for my husband, and because he drives a lot for work, at times I have a fear of him getting killed on the road. At times it has paralyzed me, and if I can't get ahold of him, I build up these ridiculous scenarios in my head. Have you been there? Maybe with your kids? It is a lie meant to take our eyes off God. I have literally talked to God in these moments and told Him that I know it isn't reality. I'll even ask Him to take it from me, but I'll pick it up again in the next thought and it takes over like a wildfire. We MUST learn to "take these thoughts captive and make them obedient to Christ." (2 Corinthians 10:5) God is FOR us; that is all we need to know. Maybe tragedy has come your way in these times, I pray you can find peace in knowing that even if the worst does happen, He loves you, He sees your grief, and you are not alone.

Verse: Isaiah 41:10
"So do not fear for I am with you, do not be dismayed for I am your God. I will strengthen you and help you. I will hold you up with my righteous right hand."

Scripture Application: Read the verse in its context. How will you apply the message of this verse to your life today?

_____

_____

_____

~~(Un)~~ Forgiven

Gratitude:

_____

_____

Affirmations: I AM STRONG. I AM FEARLESS. I AM FORGIVEN.

I AM (fill in your blank)

_____

Prayer: Heavenly Father, thank You that I don't have to live in fear. Thank You for Your strength in my weakness. Show me how to come to You, over and over when my flesh takes over and I forget that You are for me. I want to be a strong example of faith in this world. I know I fall short here; please continue to remind me who You are and Whose I am. In Jesus' name, amen.

Thoughts/Notes/Encouragement/Inspiration:

_____

_____

_____

_____

_____

DAY 18

Story: How has your faith been tested in your life? You may have been a believer your entire life, but I'm guessing at some point the thought crossed your mind that God had forgotten you or you felt disconnected from Him. I'd venture to say, if we're honest, that even the strongest of believers has struggled here. What does the word "perseverance" mean to you? To me it means my quitter won't win. No matter what happens in my life, no matter the valleys I face, I will always wake up with gratitude and praise God for all He's done in my life. We face trials because we live in a fallen world. God is not punishing you. He allows bad things to happen because He wants us to come to Him with our struggles and rely on Him to fix them so we can bring glory to Him. Your reliance on Him to fix your junk is proof to the world that your faith is bigger than your fear. Through my infertility journey, God proved Himself faithful to me even in my most broken times, the days I lay on the couch in recovery wondering why me, how was I ever going to meet a man or feel worthy when I couldn't do the thing a woman was created to do? He brought me through then. He will bring you through too. Stay in the Word, no matter what is going on in your life; the truth, His truth, WILL set you free. You will never find lack in your life, even in your darkest valley, when you give Him the first fruits of your day. You are not lacking anything, beloved, because you have the love of God in your life.

Verse: James 1:3-4

"Because you know, the testing of your faith produces perseverance. Perseverance must finish its work so that you may be mature and complete, not lacking anything."

Scripture Application: Read the verse in its context. How will you apply the message of this verse to your life today?

~~(Un)~~ Forgiven

Gratitude:

_____

_____

Affirmations: I AM GOOD. I AM GRACIOUS. I AM (fill in your blank) _____ _____

Prayer: Heavenly Father, I have been tested more times than I'd like to count, I have been frustrated, I have questioned You, I have doubted Your love for me. Please forgive me, Lord; I know You love me, I know that You will never forsake me. I know that in my darkest times You are always near. Let me rest in Your assurances today. In Jesus' name, amen.

Thoughts/Notes/Encouragement/Inspiration:

_____

_____

_____

_____

DAY 19

Story: Do you remember the story in Luke where Jesus rides into town on a donkey? People praised Jesus, they lay down palm branches and sang "Hosana in the highest!" They were excited; He had come to set them free! Although they thought it was an earthly freedom, not realizing it was a far more precious gift. He had come to die so we could all live in heaven. They were SO excited as He rode the donkey into town; it would only be a few days later they would call for His crucifixion. Oh, what fickle hearts we have, don't you agree? We feel a certain thing should be a certain way and when it's not, we turn our backs. In this case Jesus knew that it had to be that way, but in our lives, wouldn't it be easier if we stayed obedient to scripture? It's easy to praise God when life is going our way, but it's far harder to be joyful in struggle. Why is that? We KNOW that He will use our trials for His glory, so why not stay in prayer and let Him lead you through? Can you imagine the thoughts Jesus had riding into town, like, "Oh yeah, ya'll praise me now; just give it a few days." He KNEW we would disappoint Him; He knew Judas would betray Him and Peter would deny Him. He went to the cross anyway.

Verse: Luke 19:38

"Blessed is the king who comes in the name of the Lord! Peace in heaven and glory in the highest!"

Scripture Application: Read the verse in its context. How will you apply the message of this verse to your life today?

_____

_____

_____

_____

(Un) Forgiven

Gratitude:

_____

_____

Affirmations: I AM (fill in your blank)

_____

_____

Prayer: Heavenly Father, I want to glorify You in the good times and in my struggle. You gave everything for me; I want to sing Your praises when life is going my way and even when it isn't. I know You work everything for my good, even if I can't always see a way. You knew we would disappoint You then and You know it now, but You love us regardless. Let me love like You. In Jesus' name, amen.

Thoughts/Notes/Encouragement/Inspiration:

_____

_____

_____

_____

DAY 20

Story: God protects you, always. Even when you feel your most vulnerable, He protects you. He removes some people from your life; He puts others in. That comfort you feel when life is falling apart, that is Him. That peace you have when you don't think you should, that is Him. When you feel lost and broken and afraid, He is there to keep you safe. Bad things happen in this life, not because God causes them, but because we live in a fallen world. Eve ate from the tree and sin entered in. God allows bad things to happen because His hope is that we'll turn to Him and let Him make a message out of our mess. Will you give Him your mess today? You keep holding on to it when He's told you to let go. Let it go. Let Him do the work that only He can do. You're tired, you're weary. Rest easy knowing that in your deepest, darkest moments, He is there. Find HOPE in that today.

Verse: Psalm 119:114
"You are my refuge and my shield; I have put my hope in your word."

Scripture Application: Read the verse in its context. How will you apply the message of this verse to your life today?

_____

_____

_____

Gratitude:

_____

_____

_____

~~(Un)~~ Forgiven

Affirmations: I AM (fill in your blank)

_____

_____

Prayer: Heavenly Father, I don't know where I'd be without You. All my hope is in You, Jesus. When I don't know where to go, You lead me; when I don't know what to say, You give me the words; when I feel lost and scared, You protect me. You are my fortress and my rock, and I am grateful. In Jesus' name, amen.

Thoughts/Notes/Encouragement/Inspiration:

_____

_____

_____

_____

_____

DAY 21

Story: I remember the first time I knew without a doubt that God was real. My grandpa had just died. It was the worst year of my life; my grandpa was like a father to me. But I knew he was home tucked in the arms of Jesus. My grandpa wasn't sure he was going to heaven because he made too many mistakes. He met with his pastor off and on during his illness and talked with him about these things. That's the beauty of the cross; we are all sinners, we deserve a fiery death, but Jesus went to the cross as the perfect Lamb to be a sacrifice so that we can live free if we declare Him Lord of our lives. My grandpa experienced that grace. And in that moment, the worst of my life, I still had peace because I knew where He was.

Verse: Hebrews 11:1

"Now faith is being sure of what we hope for and certain of what we do not see."

Scripture Application: Read the verse in its context. How will you apply the message of this verse to your life today?

_____

_____

Gratitude:

_____

_____

~~(Un)~~ Forgiven

Affirmations: I AM HOPEFUL. I AM (fill in your blank)

_____

Prayer: Heavenly Father, thank You for revealing Your power to me in such a personal way. I crave a relationship with You, Lord, an intentional, passionate relationship. I know life gets in my way sometimes, and for that I repent. Thank You for the miracles You have performed and will perform in my life. I know I often take my faith for granted, Lord, and I don't want to. Thank You, Lord, that while I can't see You in person, I feel You inside my heart and I see You in the beauty all around. In Jesus' name, amen.

Thoughts/Notes/Encouragement/Inspiration:

_____

_____

_____

_____

_____

DAY 22

Story: Doubt. Fear. Worry. Delay and procrastination. The devil loves it when we live this way and I, even today, find myself doubting that I'll ever build the business I *know* God has called me to build. I offer that thought up to Him today. What happens between our ears isn't often truth, but when we have Jesus, we have the Holy Spirit, that still small voice, reminding us to lean into His promises instead of the fear inside.

Verse: 2 Corinthians 10:5

"We demolish arguments and every pretension that sets itself up against the knowledge of God and we take every thought captive and make it obedient to Christ."

Scripture Application: Read the verse in its context. How will you apply the message of this verse to your life today?

_____

_____

_____

Gratitude:

_____

_____

_____

_____

~~(Un)~~ Forgiven

Affirmations: I AM FREE. I AM THE HEAD AND NOT THE TAIL. I AM FORGIVEN.

I AM (fill in your blank

_____

Prayer: Heavenly Father, help me quiet the noise in my head Let me remember what You say about me and who and Whose I am. In Jesus' name, amen.

Thoughts/Notes/Encouragement/Inspiration:

_____

___

_____

___

_____

DAY 23

Story: I have filled my life with so many things that don't matter; sex, drugs, ok and some rock and roll. We have to have a little humor, don't we...I've tried to fill myself with food, exercise, diets, calorie counting, food elimination, all for selfish gain. I have left God out of my life in so many areas, often unintentionally, and even after continually meeting with Him daily, I find myself repeating selfish patterns. We hear "the spirit is willing, but the flesh is weak." (Matthew 26:41) God knows this about us; it's precisely why He sent His Son as a living sacrifice. Daily we must "take up our cross" and die to self. (Matthew 16:24) We are fleshy by nature, but when Jesus becomes the Lord of our lives, it is the Holy Spirit's conviction we feel that will lead us to the freedom in Christ we crave. You are not alone; this is a natural reaction to the flesh. Just remember that conviction means to turn from your ways, acknowledge His, and let Him make your path straight.

Verse: 2 Corinthians 7:1

"Since we have these promises, dear friends, let us purify ourselves from anything that contaminates the body and spirit, perfecting holiness out of reverence to God."

Scripture Application: Read the verse in its context. How will you apply the message of this verse to your life today?

_____

_____

_____

_____

~~(Un)~~ Forgiven

Gratitude:

_____

_____

Affirmations: I AM CLEAN IN SPIRIT. I AM HOLY. I AM CHOSEN.

I AM (fill in your blank)

_____

Prayer: Heavenly Father, thank You that I am cleansed by Your blood. Thank You for sending Your Son to die and be raised to life so that I may live eternally with You in heaven. I know I can't earn it, Lord; thank You for this gift. Let me remove anything from my life that is keeping me from living for only You. In Jesus' name, amen.

Thoughts/Notes/Encouragement/Inspiration:

_____

_____

_____

_____

_____

DAY 24

Story: Do you know the truth of the gospel? Do you know God? Intimately and personally? Are you intentionally spending quality time in the Word daily? In prayer daily? Not just going through the motions, but asking the Holy Spirit to fill you and speak to you? To truly know God, the personal, intimate relationship He craves from you is unmatched. Seek His face. Seek His truth. So many times, we have thoughts or feelings that don't align with God's truth. If it's good, it's from God; if it's not, it's a lie from the enemy. Sometimes just sitting in the right heart posture, with your hands open on your knees, asking Him to speak to you, helps to fill you up. Some days you feel it instantly; others it takes longer. Sometimes it happens later; for me it's often while I'm getting ready for my day. Be open to His "still small voice" and learn to recognize it. It's the reason I'm sitting here sharing with you today. His gentle nudge to my soul continues to put me in unfamiliar and uncomfortable situations, but my comfort is in Him, and I pray yours will be too.

Verse: John 8:32

"Then you will know the truth and the truth will set you free."

Scripture Application: Read the verse in its context. How will you apply the message of this verse to your life today?

_____

_____

_____

_____

~~(Un)~~ Forgiven

Gratitude:

_____

_____

Affirmations: I AM OPEN TO GOD'S TRUTH. I AM A SERVANT LEADER. I AM HOPEFUL.

I AM (fill in your blank)

_____

Prayer: Heavenly Father, You are the TRUTH, you are the LIFE and I know I can only come to You through Jesus. I crave Your truth, Lord; fill me with Your Spirit, today and every day. I crave the freedom that only comes from a personal, intimate relationship with my Heavenly Father. In Jesus' name, amen.

Thoughts/Notes/Encouragement/Inspiration:

_____

_____

_____

_____

_____

_____

DAY 25

Story: In the OT the Israelites had to travel to the tabernacle to commune with God; He would come in a cloud and the people could worship Him there. When Christ ascended to heaven after His death and resurrection, He sent the Holy Spirit to live in us once we accept Christ as our Lord and Savior. In that moment, our bodies become the temple of the Holy Spirit; it is our bodies that God perfects and desires for us to do His work, to love others and make disciples. We can't do that if we're unhealthy, living in the constant shame of defeat and emotional eating. Jesus walked everywhere, He was constantly on the move, eating healthy foods so He could do His ministry well, the way God called Him to. God has a calling on YOUR life as well. Do you think He likes it when we're not taking care of our bodies as He calls us to? He put clean, whole foods on this Earth for us to eat; He gave us hands and feet to move us to action. The way we eat, move, talk to ourselves, and hydrate is an act of worship. How are you treating your temple today?

Verse: Romans 12:1

"Therefore, I urge you, brothers, in view of God's mercy, to offer your bodies as a living sacrifice, holy and pleasing to God—this is your spiritual act of worship."

Scripture Application: Read the verse in its context. How will you apply the message of this verse to your life today?

_____

_____

_____

_____

~~(Un)~~ Forgiven

Gratitude:

_____

_____

Affirmations: I AM A CHAIN BREAKER. I EAT AND MOVE ACCORDING TO MY GOALS. I AM A PERSON OF ACTION.

I AM (fill in your blank)

_____

Prayer: Heavenly Father, I haven't taken very good care of my body at times. Lord, I know that I am the temple of the Holy Spirit and that it is a blessing to take a breath today, I know not everyone had that privilege. Lord, I don't want to take my body for granted; I don't want to rely on medication if there's a better way. I want to honor You with my body, my choices, and my actions. Lord, give me the discipline I need in this area to be obedient to who You need me to be. In Jesus' name, amen.

Thoughts/Notes/Encouragement/Inspiration:

_____

_____

_____

_____

_____

DAY 26

Story: Do you believe that Jesus died and was resurrected to save you from eternal hellfire? I hope so, because He did. When Jesus ascended into heaven, He sent the power of the Holy Spirit to all who believed. You have the living God inside of you. Do you realize the POWER you hold? So often, we rely on our own strength instead of letting God lead us and direct us. In our discipleship group this week, we talked about being led by the Holy Spirit, not just filled with the Holy Spirit. How can you prayerfully tap into that power right now, in this moment? Bow your head, lay your hands open on your lap and ask the Holy Spirit to come into you and do a work only He can do. Are you willing to be changed in the most POWERFUL way? I hope so! The world needs you to step into your Holy Spirit-anointed power! Will you receive it today?

Verse: John 7:38

"Whoever believes in me, as the scripture has said, streams of living water will flow from within him."

Scripture Application: Read the verse in its context. How will you apply the message of this verse to your life today?

_____

_____

_____

Gratitude:

_____

_____

~~(Un)~~ Forgiven

Affirmations: I AM WORTHY. I AM WHOLE. I AM (fill in your blank)

_____

Prayer: Heavenly Father, I know I don't say it enough, but thank You. Thank You for sending Your Son as a perfect sacrifice for an unworthy sinner. Thank You for the POWER of the cross and thank You that that power lives in me today. Come into my life, Lord, and change me in a way that only You can. In Jesus' name, amen.

Thoughts/Notes/Encouragement/Inspiration:

_____
_____
_____
_____
_____

DAY 27

Story: We were destined for hell, but Christ, in His infinite power, went to the grave and was resurrected so that we could be saved. WOW! Sometimes just reading it or saying it, we fail to comprehend it. A Man died for me and for you. He not only died, but He also rose from the dead! This is proof in the pudding that God cares for you and about you. He loves you SO MUCH that He came to Earth, lived life, and died, the perfect Lamb sacrifice. In that moment, the veil was torn, and the old covenant became new. The works of the Old Testament vanished, and Christ's ascension took its place. And even still, He sent the Holy Spirit to live IN us, so that we can have constant communication with God Himself. Yet we put Him aside and live for ourselves because we don't think He wants to be bothered with our issues. He did ALL of that and came to live in us and we STILL sometimes don't grasp the finality of what His death meant. We always have access to Him, so why do we not allow the Holy Spirit to lead us? When we work moment by moment each day to live as Christ would have us, He makes the decisions for us, and it makes life SO much easier! He only needs us to be still, to obey, yet we make it far harder on ourselves than He ever intended it to be. The proof was in the garden at the beginning, but we prove it over and over each day when we take our path instead of tapping in to His. "His mercies are new each day." (Lamentations 3:22) We have a new opportunity to seek Him. It is never too late. Are you ready to accept His gift today?

Verse: Ephesians 3:17-19 NLT

"Then Christ will make his home in your hearts as you trust in him. Your roots will grow down into God's love and keep you strong. And may you have the power to understand, as all God's people should, how wide, how long, how high, and how deep his love is. May you experience the love of Christ, though it is too great to understand fully. Then you will be made complete with all the fullness of life and power that comes from God."

~~(Un)~~ Forgiven

Scripture Application: Read the verse in its context. How will you apply the message of this verse to your life today?

_____

_____

Gratitude:

_____

_____

Affirmations: I AM (fill in your blank)

_____

_____

Prayer: Heavenly Father, sometimes it's hard for me to understand the depths of Your love. Help me today to accept the love and grace You give me, that I might extend that love and grace to others. My power comes from You, Lord, my rock, my hope, and my salvation. It's hard to put it into words sometimes, the outpouring of love I feel from Your Spirit. I am grateful today that You understand me even when I sometimes struggle to understand myself. In Jesus' name, amen.

Thoughts/Notes/Encouragement/Inspiration:

_____

_____

_____

DAY 28

Story: It is so much easier to live for ourselves, isn't it? But that isn't how scripture tells us to live. From an early age, we have an idea of what we want to do, who we want to be, and how our life "should" look, from college to marriage to kids and even the sports our kids play. So often, we leave God out of our plans, yet He WILL have His way. We can and should set goals, but WITH God. He blesses us more than we could ask or imagin;, He can do things we could never dream of doing on our own. So why do we leave Him out? I spent the better part of three decades going my own way before realizing that God will always be in control, and the sooner I get in step with Him, the better. What areas of your life are you trying to control instead of giving it up to God? Do you have a picture of your life that you've left Him out of?

Verse: Proverbs 16:9

"In his heart a man plans his course, but the Lord determines his steps."

Scripture Application: Read the verse in its context. How will you apply the message of this verse to your life today?

_____

_____

Gratitude:

_____

_____

_____

~~(Un)~~ Forgiven

Affirmations: I AM OBEDIENT. I AM SUCCESSFUL. I AM FAITHFUL.

I AM (fill in your blank)

_____

Prayer: Heavenly Father, I am grateful that I don't have to be in control, that You already have my path laid out. I know I'm a constant work in progress, Lord, and I thank You for never giving up on me. Thank You that Your path is straight and that You have my best interest at heart. In Jesus' name, amen.

Thoughts/Notes/Encouragement/Inspiration:

_____

_____

_____

_____

_____

DAY 29

Story: The Bible tells us to not fear, yet we do. Why? In this letter Paul is telling Timothy to go out and preach the good word. Timothy is a student of Paul's and Paul has been imprisoned for much of his ministry, so he was passing the torch to Timothy, who would continue Christ's teachings. Can you imagine the pressure on Timothy? Timothy was raised by his mom and grandma, who were very strong women. I can imagine the conversations they had as he was being "trained up" by Paul to go out and preach. Do you feel the spirit of fear in your life? At some point I think we all do. Do you know how to combat that fear with God's truth? Will you lean into the message of Paul, who is one of the reasons we get to worship as we do today? God takes your fear and replaces it with LOVE and SELF-DISCIPLINE. He has given us ALL we need in the Word and Holy Spirit. I know I've wasted so much time being afraid of what people will think or how I'll fail, when God isn't worried about any of that. He didn't give us fear, He gave us GOOD! How can we lean into that promise today?

Verse: 2 Timothy 1:7

"For God did not give her the spirit of fear, but the POWER of love and self-discipline." (emphasis added)

Scripture Application: Read the verse in its context. How will you apply the message of this verse to your life today?

_____

_____

_____

_____

~~(Un)~~ Forgiven

Gratitude:

_____

_____

Affirmations: I AM DISCIPLINED. I AM AT PEACE. I AM DEDICATED.

I AM (fill in your blank)

_____

Prayer: Heavenly Father, I declare myself FREE of FEAR in JESUS' NAME! I am a child of GOD! I repent of my fear and turn to You, Lord; thank You for love, for self-discipline, and all the fruits that I get to share with the people You place in my life. Let me renounce fear in all areas of my life! I trust You, Lord; I am leaning on You today. In Jesus' name, amen.

Thoughts/Notes/Encouragement/Inspiration:

_____

_____

_____

_____

_____

DAY 30

Story: It's so easy to judge the Israelites, isn't it? In Haggai we see God call them back to restore the temple and after a few weeks they go back to "paneling their own homes" or living for themselves instead of what God specifically told them to do, so He "withheld the dew and crops." (Haggai 1:10) This tells me that God expects us to be obedient and live as He's called us to. We sometimes become so focused on our lives that we forget the bigger call to make disciples. As believers, we are to die to "self" daily, to live for Christ *daily*, to pick up our cross DAILY, and follow Him. We can live for the world or for ourselves, and I don't know about you, but I'd rather be condemned by the world than by God.

Verse: Haggai 1:10

"Therefore because of you the heavens have withheld their dew and the earth its crops."

Scripture Application: Read the verse in its context. How will you apply the message of this verse to your life today?

_____

_____

Gratitude:

_____

_____

_____

_____

~~(Un)~~ Forgiven

Affirmations: I AM OBEDIENT. I AM FAITHFUL. I AM A PERSON OF ACTION.

I AM (fill in your blank)

_____

Prayer: Heavenly Father, I have been selfish, and I don't want to be. Forgive me for going my own way, Father, I repent and ask You lead me to the path You have for me and remove any distraction or selfish desire so that I can do the will You have placed in my life. In Jesus' name, amen.

Thoughts/Notes/Encouragement/Inspiration:

_____

_____

_____

_____

_____

DAY 31

Story: When I met my now husband, I remember telling him I liked him. I told him I wanted a man who would chase God with me and put me first. I remember the feeling of falling in love with him so completely it made my heart hurt to think about him not being in my life. I remember the moment God put a nudge on my heart that I needed to share. I told him that I loved him, but I loved God more and I hoped that he would feel the same. When we love God above all else, even our spouses and our kids, God brings us His best. I will always live for God first and my husband second. I pray you will find the courage to do the same. When we put God first, He makes everything better. Seek FIRST His Kingdom. "Have no other gods before me." (Exodus 20:3) "Love me above all." (Mark 12:30) The commands are clear; let us walk in this truth today.

Verse: Matthew 6:33

"But seek first His Kingdom and His righteousness and these things will be given to you as well."

Scripture Application: Read the verse in its context. How will you apply the message of this verse to your life today?

___

___

Gratitude:

___

___

___

~~(Un)~~ Forgiven

Affirmations: I AM GOD'S CHILD. I AM RIGHTEOUS. I AM HIS.

I AM (fill in your blank)

_____

Prayer: Heavenly Father, I want to seek You first in all things. Lord, remind me when life takes over and I start to go my own way that You are in control. I know that when I seek You first, life just makes sense, no matter what is going on. I can aways count on You to bring me what I need and who I need when I need it. In Jesus' name, amen.

Thoughts/Notes/Encouragement/Inspiration:

_____

_____

_____

_____

_____

_____

DAY 32

Story: Our job is to love God and love people. He calls us to care for the widows and orphans, but we focus more on our weekend plans or getting our kids to practice or our families to the next event. Where is God in our plans? How are we adopting the "serve first" mindset He calls us to? If we're blessed financially, give. If we're blessed with time, serve. If we're blessed with a big home or car, host. We are all called in different capacities; ALL work together for the good of His Kingdom, but we need to remove the selfishness from our schedules and seek to serve first. What does serving look like to you? Do you feel He's calling you to serve in a specific way? Are you being obedient to that call? What sort of activities do you always make time for and what sort of activities you've maybe been called to that you always make excuses for? We will ALL answer for our actions or lack thereof. If we're more concerned about our plans instead of serving others and sharing the gospel, we need to seriously reprioritize our lives.

Verse: Philippians 2:1

"If you have any encouragement from being united with Christ, if any comfort from His love, if any fellowship with the Spirit, if any tenderness and compassion, then make my joy complete by being like-minded, having the same love, being in one spirit and purpose."

Scripture Application: Read the verse in its context. How will you apply the message of this verse to your life today?

_____

_____

_____

_____

~~(Un)~~ Forgiven

Gratitude:

_____

_____

Affirmations: I AM SAVED. I AM FOCUSED. I AM (fill in your blank)

_____

Prayer: Heavenly Father, I know I focus more on my plans than Yours; help me to do what You need me to do. Help me to say yes to what You expect from me instead of my selfish desires. Help me to take up my cross daily so I can be who You need me to be. Let me release my selfishness and fear and show me who I need to be in You by my love of other people. You call me to love and serve and make disciples, and I want to be obedient; help me, Father. In Jesus' name, amen.

Thoughts/Notes/Encouragement/Inspiration:

_____

_____

_____

_____

_____

_____

DAY 33

Story: You are APPOINTED. You are ANNOINTED. You have a DIVINE calling on your life and it's time to get moving! You have what you need; stop waiting. You will NEVER be ready. He doesn't need you to be; He needs you to OBEY. Our minds tell us we're not enough, our "feelings" dictate our emotions. Pray through the noise, seek His face, and let the peace that passes all understanding guard and guide you. He will always equip you for where He calls you. You are never alone; you are always covered. I hope that fires you UP for all God has in store for your life! Pray through your doubt and insecurity, ask for the Holy Spirit's guidance, let Him by His power lead you down the path. You are the vessel; He is the key. You don't need to be ready or qualified, you only need to be obedient and courageous, and He'll give you the discipline for that too! Are you ready to be His vessel no matter how you "feel?" I know the power procrastination has on a mind; I put off writing this book for years. Recently God put on my heart Obedience > Outcome. He doesn't need us to know it all or be who we "think" we need to be. We need to be the vessel, ready and willing to go where He calls. What are you afraid of? Use the area below to write out your fears, then pray over them. Ask God to remove them from your mind and replace them with the discipline to move and the steps to get there. Watch how He provides!

Verse: 1 Timothy 1:12

"I thank Christ Jesus our Lord, who has given me strength, that he considered me faithful, appointing me to his service."

Scripture Application: Read the verse in its context. How will you apply the message of this verse to your life today?

_____

_____

~~(Un)~~ Forgiven

Gratitude:

_____

_____

Affirmations: I AM ANNOINTED. I AM APPOINTED. I AM (fill in your blank)

_____

Prayer: Heavenly Father, I am empty; I have nothing without You. You are my strength and for that I am grateful. Renew my spirit today, Lord, and let me be obedient to Your call. I am here to serve and not to be served, I am here to step out in faith to do Your will. Even if it makes me uncomfortable and I don't feel qualified, I know that You will always give me what I need. In Jesus' name, amen.

Thoughts/Notes/Encouragement/Inspiration:

_____

_____

_____

_____

_____

DAY 34

Story: When we're tempted with sin, we must set our eyes on things above. Gossip and inappropriate television or music, even memes on social media, we can be tempted to watch or laugh or partake of when we know it's not who God has called us to be. The closer you get to God, the more these things will start to weigh on you. That's Holy Spirit conviction and it is not to be ignored. We are called for a higher purpose, clearer direction, and to be set apart. We worry more about what people think about us than we do about God. If we don't laugh at an inappropriate joke people will think we're weird, if we don't order a drink when everyone else does we're a prude, or when we eat a salad when everyone else is eating pizza, we're too healthy. What I'll say about all of that is that if you're living out your conviction because of Holy Spirit conviction then anyone else's opinion doesn't matter, I don't care who's it is. Your ONLY job in this life is to live for God, not the world or your flesh. Stand strong in your conviction today; you are not alone!

Verse: Hebrews 12:2

"Let us fix our eyes on Jesus, the author and perfector of our faith, who for the joy set before him endured the cross, scorning it's shame and sat down at the right hand of the throne of God."

Scripture Application: Read the verse in its context. How will you apply the message of this verse to your life today?

_____

_____

Gratitude:

_____

_____

~~(Un)~~ Forgiven

Affirmations: I AM (fill in your blank)

_____

_____

Prayer: Heavenly Father, thank You for going to the cross for me. Thank You for saving me from myself and my sin. Thank You for living inside of me and that I can chat with You all the time. I crave a personal, intimate relationship with You, Lord. How can I live for You today? Show me all You have for me and let me release all my fear and step into the plan and purpose You have for my life. In Jesus' name, amen.

Thoughts/Notes/Encouragement/Inspiration:

_____

_____

_____

_____

_____

_____

DAY 35

Story: A few of my clients and friends spent a month in the book of Haggai; it always amazes me how God makes stories that are thousands of years old relevant today. Basically, Haggai the prophet called God's people to rebuild Solomon's temple after it was destroyed. At first everyone was excited and focused, then after a time, the excitement wore off. I love this story. This is a great lesson for new clients especially, because like any healthy plan, it's great at first but then life happens, and we don't see what we want to right away, so we make excuses and quit. So, what did God do in Haggai? He withheld their blessings. He called them out: "You have planted much but harvested little." (Haggai 1:6) Have you been there? I have. We never have enough of all we think we're due, finances are never enough even when you have everything you need, you're always hungry or wanting the next drink. Want. Want. Want. When God calls us, we need to be obedient. Not because He may withhold our blessings, but because He is God, and we are not. We've got to start making uncomfortable decisions because He tells us to and stop living in "selfish motives or vain conceit." (Philippians 2:3) Thankfully, after Haggai calls out the people, they resume their work and God restores their blessings. But wouldn't it be nice if He didn't have to withhold blessings in the first place and we just worked because He said to? I want to be that kind of obedient, don't you?

Verse: Haggai 1:5-6

"Give careful thought to your ways, you have planted much but harvested little. You eat but never have enough, you drink but never have your fill. You put on clothes but are not warm. You earn wages, only to put them in a purse with holes in it."

~~(Un)~~ Forgiven

Scripture Application: Read the verse in its context. How will you apply the message of this verse to your life today?

_____

_____

Gratitude:

_____

_____

Affirmations: I AM (fill in your blank)

_____

_____

Prayer: Heavenly Father, I have worked to glorify myself instead of You. Forgive me. I ache to live for You, my only HOPE is in You, Lord, yet I seem determined to make my own path. I offer my life to You in this moment. Create a change in me that only You can, I don't want to waste the blessings of my life. I am here, I am willing; thank You for new mercies each day. In Jesus' name, amen.

Thoughts/Notes/Encouragement/Inspiration:

_____

_____

_____

_____

DAY 36

Story: Do you see struggles as an opportunity to grow? There are always ways to improve in the valley. What do you see down there? In the valley is where the stream flows and the flowers grow; in the valley is where we're taken to our knees in prayer. The valley is where we realize God's power in our lives; it's where the fruit is cultivated. The valley may not be present at the time, but I promise that if you continue to glorify God in ALL circumstances of your life, He will not only bring you out of it, but He will also make you into someone you don't even recognize. I have learned this lesson over and over. Sure, the peak of the mountain feels good, but I think most of life is overcoming challenges and realizing that we were never meant to face them alone. Life may be steady for a time, but a challenge will arise. When we give God our junk, our worst-case scenario, He sometimes lovingly must force us to obedience. "No discipline is pleasant at the time but painful. Later on, however, it produces a harvest of righteousness and peace for those who are trained by it." (Hebrews 12:11) Do you remember that verse in Hebrews we read earlier? Righteousness and peace, what a beautiful reward.

Verse: Hebrews 12:7

"Endure hardship as discipline. God is treating you as sons, for what son is not disciplined by his father."

Scripture Application: Read the verse in its context. How will you apply the message of this verse to your life today?

_____

_____

_____

~~(Un)~~ Forgiven

Gratitude:

_____

_____

Affirmations: I AM (fill in your blank)

_____

_____

Prayer: Heavenly Father, this is a hard one for me. I want to grow in my struggles, Lord, but I am frustrated. Show me the blessing in this time, let my struggle glorify You and let every person who is involved see You in the good of this process, including myself. I have overcome so much because of Your precious grace, and I know I will again. Let me not give in to the temptation to be bitter or angry, but let me see this as You changing me from the inside out as I have asked. In Jesus' name, amen.

Thoughts/Notes/Encouragement/Inspiration:

_____

_____

_____

_____

_____

DAY 37

Story: When I decided to build a business in 2017, I had no idea how God would use the "personal development" aspect to bring me closer and closer to Him. Seeking His will above my own has become a daily intention. And while I often miss the mark or my flesh takes over, He is always there to redirect me and bring me back. I envision a future full of women so focused on Holy Spirit conviction they can't HELP but see themselves as God does: loved, chosen, healed, beautiful, and forgiven. I refuse to give up on the conviction He has placed in my heart. I may not be able to see a way, but He does and that's all I need. Will you continue to lean in when the road feels weary and you're not sure how to continue?

Verse: Galatians 6:9

"Let us not grow weary in doing good, for at the proper time we will reap harvest if we do not give up."

Scripture Application: Read the verse in its context. How will you apply the message of this verse to your life today?

_____

_____

Gratitude:

_____

_____

_____

~~(Un)~~ Forgiven

Affirmations: I AM HEALED. I AM BEAUTIFUL. I AM FORGIVEN. I AM (fill in your blank)

_____

Prayer: Heavenly Father, I am weary, but I am ready. I don't see a way, Lord, but You do. I am here, I am ready, I ache to bring glory to You through my work, my life, my relationships, and my finances, Lord. Lead me in every area of my life. In Jesus' name, amen.

Thoughts/Notes/Encouragement/Inspiration:

_____

_____

_____

_____

_____

_____

_____

DAY 38

Story: I gained 100 pounds. From following yo-yo, keto style diets to suffering deep depression after the loss of my grandfather, I was "overweight physically and underweight spiritually," as Lysa Terkeurst says. When you have God as the ruler of your life, you have the fruits of the Spirit, one of them being self-discipline. It's in us; we must cultivate it and it IS painful, as scripture says. But we are worthy; I am and so are you. Seeking God's strength in every area of life is required for success, but especially in self-discipline, as it applies to so many areas of our lives.

Verse: Hebrews 12:11

"No discipline is pleasant at the time but painful, later on however, it produces a harvest of righteousness and peace for those who are trained by it."

Scripture Application: Read the verse in its context. How will you apply the message of this verse to your life today?

_____

_____

Gratitude:

_____

_____

_____

_____

~~(Un)~~ Forgiven

Affirmations: I AM DISCIPLINED. I AM ORGANIZED. I AM PRODUCTIVE. I AM (fill in your blank)

_____

Prayer: Heavenly Father, thank You for the fruits of the Spirit, and thank You most for the spirit of discipline. I know I can't do anything on my own, Lord, but with You I can do ALL things, even cultivate new habits. Give me strength and direction, Father. In Jesus' name, amen.

Thoughts/Notes/Encouragement/Inspiration:

_____

_____

_____

_____

_____

_____

_____

DAY 39

Story: Ugh, this can be SO hard, can't it? It's not supposed to be; as believers God gives us what we need. Then some shiny thing comes and BAM! We're distracted and thrown off course,; tell me I'm not alone here. I've been distracted by diets and men and TV shows. Even GOOD things can become distractions or idols if we're not careful. Sugar is a big one for me; it's hard to go anywhere these days where sugar isn't, and we're often pressured to "try this or that." How do we stay true to our convictions when God has told us to refrain? We like sugar; we don't want to look weird when everyone else is enjoying a treat. And don't get me wrong, I'm not saying don't enjoy it on occasion if you want to; I'm just saying that at times, God will ask you to give it up, like He has been for me recently and I have not been obedient. What do we want more? The 10 second adrenaline rush to please our senses or to please God? This applies to so many areas of life; this is just the one I'm facing currently, and I imagine some of you may be too.

Verse: Romans 12:2

"Do not be conformed to the pattern of the world any longer but be transformed by the renewing of your mind."

Scripture Application: Read the verse in its context. How will you apply the message of this verse to your life today?

Gratitude:

~~(Un)~~ Forgiven

Affirmations: I AM A CHILD OF GOD. I AM A SURVIVOR. I WILL OVERCOME.

I AM (fill in your blank)

_____

Prayer: Heavenly Father, it isn't always easy to say no to cravings, however they look in the moment, but I know You've given me prayer and the fruits to combat the lies that the world puts into my head. Fill me with Your truth today, give me the discipline I need to fight my cravings, and let me live only for You and Your will for my life. In Jesus' name, amen.

Thoughts/Notes/Encouragement/Inspiration:

_____

_____

_____

_____

_____

_____

DAY 40

Story: If you only give 50%, you'll get 50%. If you give 80, you'll get 80. Even if five days out of seven is only a "C" average, is that the life you hope for? Is that the example you hope to set? I think not. We all have seven days in the week and 24 hours in the day; give yourself WHOLLY to them. Every day won't be amazing; to be honest, we're all probably in the 55%-70% range most days, but whatever you have that day, give your all! I tell clients that if you only follow your meal plan through the week and go all out on the weekends, you're only earning about a "C" average. Is that the grade you want? Is that a grade your kids could bring home that you'd celebrate? I don't think so. When God calls you, GO ALL IN! Of course, you'll have struggle days and days that fall apart, it's normal, but you can still give Him what you DO have that day. He doesn't require or expect perfection, but He does, in my opinion, expect you to try and to give what you have. He takes over where we fall short, so giving what you do have allows glory to go to Him when you make it through the day successfully, even if that means you didn't get a shower and your work is only half done. Consistency over time is what creates results, but a constant C" average... I think God deserves better than that, and beloved, so do you.

Verse: 1 Timothy 4:15

"Be diligent in these matters; give yourself wholly to them, so that everyone may see your progress."

Scripture Application: Read the verse in its context. How will you apply the message of this verse to your life today?

_____

_____

_____

~~(Un)~~ Forgiven

Gratitude:

_____

_____

Affirmations: I AM CONSISTENT. I AM WORTH THE WORK. I AM GOD'S MASTERPIECE.

I AM (fill in your blank)

_____

_____

Prayer: Heavenly Father, I want to honor You with my choices; show me how I can do that today. I want people to see Your light shine through me, I want to give you glory in all things. Give me the strength I need to start, the disciple to keep going when it gets hard, and the perseverance to push when I want to quit. In Jesus' name, amen.

Thoughts/Notes/Encouragement/Inspiration:

_____

_____

_____

_____

Lindy Schlabach

DAY 41

Story: Motivation doesn't exist, in my opinion. You must be willing to do the work it takes to become the person you want to become, and that comes from cultivating a spirit of discipline. You have it, scripture says so. I hear from clients all the time that they're "not motivated." I agree. I rarely am either, but I AM DISCIPLINED, because I take steps DAILY to make it happen. Building discipline, according to a Google search, takes a minimum of 64 days and up to three years. I like to say those are worldly standards and we don't live by those; we live by the power of God's Word, and He says you have discipline already, so how do you take steps daily to get there? What's helped me is 1. Praying over my goals and asking God to give me specifics. 2. Plan. Failing to plan is planning to fail. Set a deadline, then work backwards. If it's a weight loss goal by a certain date, you know you have X number of weeks to accomplish it and 1-2 pounds lost weekly is healthy and sustainable. Let's say we have 10 weeks left to lose six pounds; we can easily work backwards to formulate a plan weekly/daily. 3. DAILY action plan. One to three steps that will help me move towards my goal. -Find a workout I can do with my schedule. -A meal plan, not an elimination diet, that will keep me focused, full and satiated. -Accountability is key for me; it's why I became a coach. I was able to stay focused more easily on my goals when I had women cheering me on. -Grace. What happens if I do reach my goal? What happens if I don't? DISCIPLINE IS A FRUIT OF THE SPIRIT. You have what you need when you have Jesus! Lean into the Word FIRST and let Him move you forward!

Verse: Hebrews 12:11

"No discipline is pleasant at the time, but painful. Later on, however, it produces a harvest of righteousness and peace for those who are trained by it."

~~(Un)~~ Forgiven

Scripture Application: Read the verse in its context. How will you apply the message of this verse to your life today?

_____

_____

Gratitude:

_____

_____

Affirmations: I AM ACTIVE. I AM DISCIPLINED. I AM (fill in your blank)

_____

Prayer: Heavenly Father, thank You for the spirit of discipline and that I get to be a person of action. Thank You for helping me to cultivate this habit so I can be all and do all You have for me. I know I make excuses, Lord, and I ask for forgiveness. I know that building new disciplines is tricky, but with You I can do all things! In Jesus' name, amen.

Thoughts/Notes/Encouragement/Inspiration:

_____

_____

_____

_____

DAY 42

Story: Do you make time to read the Bible every day? I hope so. It is the guidebook to life. The answer to every question you'll ever face is in there. Ask God to lead you where to read. Read one to three verses a day if you have trouble comprehending it all. Do you know the story of Abraham? Abraham and Sarah begged God for a child. He had promised them a child, but Sarah was in a hurry; she was very old, so she had Abraham sleep with her maidservant. Hagar had Ishmael and Sarah got jealous. She and Abraham didn't like God's timetable, so they worked on their own. Can you relate? Have you been in a hurry to do something or be someone that God hasn't told you to be? Are you wishing for a position you're not qualified to hold? I have! I've been there more times than I can count; I'm there now if I'm being honest. God STILL used Abraham and He will still use you! Jesus is a direct descendant from Abraham's line! How amazing is that!? That is God's grace, and it is free to anyone who desires a personal relationship with Him. When I read these stories in the Bible I always ask, "Okay, Lord, how can I apply the lesson of this story to my life today?" If you look at who God used in the Bible, they were all imperfect people who fell short daily. Yet He used them to accomplish His plans. I hope you find comfort here, as I have. Your past, your hurt, your struggles can all be used to glorify His Kingdom when you work to glorify Him in everything you do.

Verse: Acts 13:23

"From this man's descendants God has brought Israel the Savior Jesus as He promised."

Scripture Application: Read the verse in its context. How will you apply the message of this verse to your life today?

_____

_____

~~(Un)~~ Forgiven

Gratitude:

_____

_____

Affirmations: I AM (fill in your blank)

_____

Prayer: Heavenly Father, thank You for the stories of the Bible. Thank You for showing me where I came from. Thank You, Lord, for the intricate creation of the Bible and how it weaves in and out and back and forth from Old to New Testament, for Your promises and hope fulfilled in the lives of the prophets and Your servants. Thank You for delicately creating every person in the Bible who has a part to play in the miracle of Jesus. Thank You for Your written Word; let me spend time learning all You have for me to learn, Lord. I know not everyone in the world has access to a Bible, Lord; let me not take mine for granted. I don't want dust to sit on it, but I want to be in it every day. Remind me that it's my guidebook for life. Lord, I thank you for its promises today. In Jesus' name, amen.

Thoughts/Notes/Encouragement/Inspiration:

_____

_____

_____

_____

DAY 43

Story: God gives us a way out of temptation through the Holy Spirit. At any time, in any situation, you can send a silent prayer up to Him and He will provide the way. This past weekend I spent with family. There are always ridiculous amounts of sweets around and I had already committed to one treat per day; we were gone for two. I prayed. I stayed away from where the treats were, and I am proud to say that He delivered! Day two I walked past a table with a homemade sugar cookie (my favorite) with a maple frosting (my double favorite) and my body literally pulled me to that table. He moved me away. I felt a physical pull to that cookie. Have you been there? It's like your body is on its own and you must have that right now! But you don't have to! And you shouldn't, if that's an area He's convicted you. There are times where I treat myself, but right now, in this season, it isn't one of them, so I am working to be obedient to where He's called me. It is not easy, but most things in life worth having aren't easy. You CAN beat a sugar craving; you can overcome disordered eating! I see it with my clients all the time! Seek His face and let Him remove that temptation from you. In those desperate moments, walking away from that cookie will feel SO victorious, you won't be able to wait until you can do it again!

Verse: 1 Corinthians 10:13

"No temptation has seized you except what is common to man. And God is faithful He will not let you be tempted beyond what you can bear."

Scripture Application: Read the verse in its context. How will you apply the message of this verse to your life today?

_____

_____

_____

~~(Un)~~ Forgiven

Gratitude:

_____

_____

Affirmations: I AM (fill in your blank)\

_____

Prayer: Heavenly Father, You are all I need. I release all my cravings to You. I release my fear and doubt, I release ideas of having to look or be a certain way. I have placed too much stock in things of this world, Lord, and I repent and ask that You change me from the inside out. I want to crave only You, Lord; You are all I need. Thank You for the fruit of self-control. In Jesus' name, amen.

Thoughts/Notes/Encouragement/Inspiration:

_____

_____

_____

_____

_____

_____

DAY 44

Story: Only God can hear our thoughts, the enemy cannot. The second negativity or gossip or unkind words come out of your mouth, the enemy clings to them. The enemy cannot be all places at once; he is not God. God is omnipresent and omniscient; He is everywhere all the time. The enemy has evil cohorts who torment us at times, but sometimes the fear and doubt we face are from our own self-sabotage. We must learn to combat the lies of the enemy and of our flesh with the truth of the gospel. If we say "I am fat. I am tired. I am angry" we become those things. If we say, "I am healthy. I am happy. I am joyful. I move and eat according to God's will for my life," we become those things. What we say is what we cling to or what the enemy clings to. Speak only good, about yourselves and others. Loving your neighbor as you love yourself is tough when you don't always love yourself. Start speaking kindness to your body and to others, out loud, and see the kind of good fruit God brings into your life. If what we reap is what we sow, shouldn't we always be sowing good seeds?' I hope so.

Verse: Romans 12:9-10

"Love must be sincere, hate what is evil and cling to what is good. Be devoted to one another in brotherly love. Honor one another above yourselves."

Scripture Application: Read the verse in its context. How will you apply the message of this verse to your life today?

_____

_____

_____

_____

~~(Un)~~ Forgiven

Gratitude:

_____

_____

Affirmations: I AM (fill in your blank)

_____

Prayer: Heavenly Father, sometimes I forget that it isn't people that are evil but that some are overtaken by the enemy. I know that everything and everyone You made is good. I want to focus on the good, the good in the world and the good in people; remind me of my shortcomings so I can have the grace for others that You have for me. In Jesus' name, amen.

Thoughts/Notes/Encouragement/Inspiration:

_____

_____

_____

_____

_____

_____

DAY 45

Story: What do you need? Like, actually need. Food. Water. Shelter? When you say, "Oh. I need that!" what is that? Is it something you need? We know Jesus lived in the dessert fasting for 40 days. He didn't' need food, He needed communion with God. God meets every need. We read in scripture how He clothed the flowers and gave the birds what they need; why do we think we "need" the newest iPhone or leggings your friend has? We need to fast. We need to pray. We need to love and serve people and make disciples; the rest is what we want. In scripture, we read where Jesus says, *"when"* you fast, not *"if"* you fast; do you see the difference? He implies that it is expected. I've never felt closer to God than when I've fasted; the outline for this book came from a fast. You can fast from many things: food, social media, sugar, something you've come to rely on that maybe isn't serving you, like coffee or a snack you look forward to. Fasting is trusting that God will always meet your needs and in that time of extreme hunger, when you bow your head in reverence, He fills you, restores you and strengthens you. Fasting breaks chains, and it is a discipline I believe more Christians should align with.

Verse: Philippians 4:19

"And my God will meet all your needs according to His glorious riches in Christ Jesus."

Scripture Application: Read the verse in its context. How will you apply the message of this verse to your life today?

_____

_____

_____

_____

~~(Un)~~ Forgiven

Gratitude:

_____

_____

Affirmations: I AM HEALTHY. I AM OBEDIENT. I AM GRATEFUL.

I AM (fill in your blank)

_____

Prayer: Heavenly Father, thank You for fulfilling every need I have. Father, reveal to me anything that isn't of You and let me leave it behind. Continue to speak to me, Lord, and lead me down the path You have chosen for me. You give me everything I need, and I am so grateful. In Jesus' name, amen.

Thoughts/Notes/Encouragement/Inspiration:

_____

_____

_____

_____

_____

_____

DAY 46

Story: As previously mentioned, Jesus doesn't say "if" you fast, He says "WHEN" you fast. Fasting is an expected spiritual discipline and one that may feel uncomfortable at first, but I'm telling you, you will come to enjoy it. Fasting is a way to connect with God on a much deeper level. I have fasted from food, but I have also fasted from other things as well. Both are beneficial, but fasting food is what, I believe, Jesus calls us to. Start small, maybe a16-24 hour fast. I drink water and coffee; some people just drink water. Some people can't physically fast and that's okay; maybe try a caffeine fast or social media fast. If there's something you rely on each day, fast from that, but if you can fast from food, I recommend it. The day before a fast you should eat lightly, the evening before have a small meal and nothing too fatty, maybe a salad or some raw veggies with protein and a potato. In those times of sincere hunger, bow your head to pray, ask God to fill you with what He has for you. Seek His face. One thing I did during my first fast was watch The Passion of the Christ. Jesus sacrificed His LIFE for us; I can give up food for a few days. Lean in. Don't tell people you're fasting except those who need to know so they can pray for you. The objective is to get closer to God, not to seek glory from the world. Have you fasted? Will you commit to this spiritual discipline?

Verse: Matthew 6:16

"When you fast, do not look somber as the hypocrites do, for they disfigure their faces to show men they're fasting. I tell you the truth, they have received their reward in full."

Scripture Application: Read the verse in its context. How will you apply the message of this verse to your life today?

_____

_____

~~(Un)~~ Forgiven

Gratitude:

_____

_____

Affirmations: I AM (fill in your blank)

_____

Prayer: Heavenly Father, I want to be obedient in the call to fast, but I am scared. I don't know what I'm doing, but I know in scripture You expect us to fast. Show me how, show me when, show me all You have for me and let me connect with You in a way that I've never felt before. I am excited to take on a new spiritual discipline. I know that my flesh is weak, but with You in me, Lord, I can do ALL things. In Jesus' name, amen.

Thoughts/Notes/Encouragement/Inspiration:

_____

_____

_____

_____

Lindy Schlabach

DAY 47

Story: I got married at 40 and I won't lie, it was hard, it's still hard. Neither of us had been married before or lived with anyone. We live together very well, but there were some things we had to work through. We always joke that we don't know how people stay married without God, as hard as it is WITH Him in our lives. When we relinquish control and truly TRUST that God IS in control, He gives us the things we need to become the people we need to be so that we can do all we need to do. You may have an issue with a family member or coworker, child, or even spouse, whoever it may be, give it up to God, and ask Him to reveal any areas of your life you need to acknowledge that are keeping you from being who He needs you to be. So often we ask God to change the other person when we really need to change ourselves. I had to work through some serious control issues and false humility and while it doesn't feel good to admit that, I can't be who God needs me to be, therefore who my husband needs me to be if I'm not willing to do the work required.

Verse: 2 Peter 1: 5-6 NIV

"For this very reason, make every effort to add to your faith goodness and to goodness, knowledge and to knowledge, self-control and to self-control perseverance and to perseverance godliness and to godliness, brotherly kindness and to brotherly kindness, love."

Scripture Application: Read the verse in its context. How will you apply the message of this verse to your life today?

_____

_____

_____

~~(Un)~~ Forgiven

Gratitude:

_____

_____

Affirmations: I AM LOVED. I AM HEALED. I AM WHOLE.

I AM (fill in your blank)

_____

Prayer: Heavenly Father, thank You for the blessing of continually growing in You. Let me love as You love and lead as You lead. You have given me everything I need, Lord; let me use these gifts to bless others and be the example You need me to be. You call me to love people and make disciples. Father, let me do these things as You wish. In Jesus' name, amen.

Thoughts/Notes/Encouragement/Inspiration:

_____

_____

_____

_____

_____

_____

DAY 48

Story: Do you realize that before Genesis 1, God knew you? He did. He knew every hair on your head, every struggle you'd face and the strength you'd carry. He named you before the world even existed,; that alone should be proof that you matter, that you have purpose, and that you are loved. Maybe you never received loved at home or school or in your relationships, but God loves you, more that you can even imagine, and He knows the struggle you're facing to live the purpose He has for you. He wants you to know that He sees you, He hears you, and He is there for you. Look up, say His name, let His love rain down upon you, and let His light shine through all you do in your life, your work, your relationships. He has a plan for you. If you're still searching, seek His guidance and let Him show you all He has for your life. You will rarely "feel" worthy, but remember that your feelings aren't always valid. Who does God say you are? Lean on THAT promise and you'll always shine!

Verse: Ephesians 2:10

"For we are God's masterpiece. Created anew in Christ Jesus to do good works, which God prepared us in advance to do."

Scripture Application: Read the verse in its context. How will you apply the message of this verse to your life today?

_____

_____

_____

_____

_____

~~(Un)~~ Forgiven

Gratitude:

_____

_____

Affirmations: I AM CHOSEN. I AM GENTLE. I AM A CHILD OF THE MOST HIGH GOD.

I AM (fill in your blank)

_____

Prayer: Heavenly Father, I know You have a plan for me. Please show me the areas where I need to improve, lead me to Your perfect plan, and if I need any kind of direction, Lord, direct me today. In Jesus' name, amen.

Thoughts/Notes/Encouragement/Inspiration:

_____

_____

_____

_____

_____

_____

_____

DAY 49

Story: I was 100 pounds overweight and cried through exercise, yet today, I am a fitness and nutrition coach working with women, helping them seek God in their journey to healthy living. Only God! If you'd told me 10 years ago that this is where I'd be, I'd have laughed you out of the house. Today, God still redirects the path I started out on all those years ago when I first said "yes" to this opportunity. He has molded me and shaped me along the way. Almost seven years later, I continue to be amazed at how He uses this business to shape me. It started out as a way for me to help people, yet I am the one who is continuously inspired and changed by them. What if I'd said no or waited? God has turned me upside down so many times in my business, because of my flesh that keeps trying to take over. He keeps reminding me WHY I'm here. I want to see every woman everywhere push past fear and step into God's plan for her life so she can impact change and help others do the same, to make disciples and encourage them to do the same. Isn't that the call? Don't give up, and even if it sounds or feels crazy, if it came from God, trust that He will do an amazing work through you! Where He calls, He equips!

Verse: Romans 8:28

"And we know that in all things, God works for the good of those who love Him, who have been called according to His purpose."

Scripture Application: Read the verse in its context. How will you apply the message of this verse to your life today?

_____

_____

_____

~~(Un)~~ Forgiven

Gratitude:

_____

_____

Affirmations: I AM A CHANGE MAKER. I AM A HOPE DEALER. I AM A DISCIPLE MAKER.

I AM (fill in your blank)

_____

Prayer: Heavenly Father, I know You have a plan for me, Lord, I feel it in my soul. Show me what You have for me today. Lord, I don't know how I'll do it, but I know that You'll give me everything I need! Let me not live in fear of the unknown but in faith, knowing that wherever You call me, You will also equip me! In Jesus' name, amen.

Thoughts/Notes/Encouragement/Inspiration:

_____

_____

_____

DAY 50

Story: Do you believe you're here for a purpose? Do you know what your purpose is? Do you feel an ache inside you that pulls you towards a certain type of work? Do you believe that God put you here with divine purpose and that the call on your life is to make disciples wherever you go? Because He did, and that's exactly what He calls you to do. For some people it may be more glamorous, but for others it could be in serving at a local restaurant or volunteer work. It could be speaking on stage or working with kids. It could be writing a book or building a business. You KNOW the nudge you feel; stop ignoring it. Pray over it and let Him tell you where to go, what to, do and how to do it. I've always felt the nudge to write, but I had no idea what it would look like. After a fast, He provided the outline, verses, and tools; He gives me every word as I sit here typing. Your life is a living sacrifice just as Jesus' was and you, beloved, have the same power, MORE POWER as the Word says that Jesus did on the cross! Do you believe that? Scripture says it is so, so I hope you do! I pray that you will seek the courage to MOVE, however He calls you to move. Leave the fear behind; you are a LIGHT shining on a HILL! Your sin cannot stop you unless you allow it; repent, and move forward. He can use the junk of your past to be the message of your future!

Verse: Matthew 5:14-16

"You are the light of the world, a city on a hill cannot be hidden. Neither do people light a lamp and put it under a bowl. Instead, they put it on its stand, and it gives light to everyone in the house. In the same way, let your light shine before men, that they may see your good deeds and praise your Father in heaven."

Scripture Application: Read the verse in its context. How will you apply the message of this verse to your life today?

_____

_____

~~(Un)~~ Forgiven

Gratitude:

_____

_____

Affirmations: I AM LIGHT. I AM COURAGEOUS. I SHINE BRIGHT.

I AM (fill in your blank)

_____

Prayer: Heavenly Father, I ache to be light in a dark world. Show me all You have for me, Father. Your Word says that the POWER of the resurrected Christ lives in me! That excites me for all that is to come. I don't want to blend into the world. I want people to see You shine through me in every area of my life. You've given me everything, Lord; show me how to shine for You today. In Jesus' name, amen.

Thoughts/Notes/Encouragement/Inspiration:

_____

_____

_____

_____

_____

Lindy Schlabach

DAY 51

Story: I was a binge drinker for years. After my sexual assault I fell into extreme partying and sexual promiscuity; I was searching for anything that would comfort me or fill me. I was baptized at 14 but I'd turned so far from God, I didn't think He'd want me back. I was determined to make it on my own. For 15 years alcohol, sex, food, and a good high were my constant, until I heard a new message of redemption and grace. Jesus loves you. He died for you. He died the most horrible, painful death so that we could live free, yet we try everything else first. I wish I'd have heard this message as a teen; maybe I wouldn't have wasted so much time. We are sinners by nature, but His resurrection means LIFE for anyone who chooses to believe. My salvation is my greatest gift and my prayer for you, if you're seeking something to fill you, is that you'd ask God to reveal Himself to you in such a way that you KNOW, without a shadow of a doubt, that He loves you and is calling you home. His peace passes ALL understanding; we don't get how or why it works and we don't have to. We get to walk in the light of His glorious gift. If you haven't already, will you accept it today?

Verse: 1 Peter 2:11

"Dear friends, I urge you, as aliens and strangers in the world, to abstain from sinful desires, which war against your soul."

Scripture Application: Read the verse in its context. How will you apply the message of this verse to your life today?

_____

_____

~~(Un)~~ Forgiven

Gratitude:

_____

_____

Affirmations: I AM STRONG. I AM DISCIPLINED. I AM GENTLE.

I AM (fill in your blank)

_____

Prayer: Heavenly Father, give me the strength I need today to stay away from the things that don't serve me. Show me what You have for me today and remove the rest from my life, Lord. I know I am a sinner, redeemed by Your grace alone, the greatest gift I've ever received. Thank You for the strength to turn away from the things You don't want for me. In Jesus' name, amen.

Thoughts/Notes/Encouragement/Inspiration:

_____

_____

_____

_____

_____

_____

DAY 52

Story: "Repent and you will be saved." (Acts 3:19) Do you repent daily? I hope so. My friend Leah shared the PRAY acronym with me and the 'R' was a huge area I was neglecting. P-Praise Him and all He's done and will do. 'R'-repent. 'A'-ask for others 'Y'-ask for yourself. I find most days my 'R' is the longest part of my prayer, after 'P.' It isn't enough to just repent, however; we must ask God to CHANGE us. Father, reveal to me my innermost struggles and let me be CHANGED by Holy Spirit power. In the Made to Crave 60-day devotional, Lysa's first day is titled, "Unsettle Me" and that is a prayer I pray often. We must be changed by the gospel; we must be willing to release every part of us that we have and be willing to become who He needs us to become. That starts with true repentance and desire to live changed by the Holy Spirit living in us. We are God's masterpiece; we were created with divine purpose so we must always be leaning into the Word to become the agents of change He desires for us to be! Do you repent daily? Do you actively work to change according to gospel teachings?

Verse: James 5:16

"Therefore, confess your sins to each other and pray for each other so that you may be healed. The prayer of a righteous man is powerful and effective."

Scripture Application: Read the verse in its context. How will you apply the message of this verse to your life today?

_____

_____

_____

~~(Un)~~ Forgiven

Gratitude:

_____

_____

Affirmations: I AM A PRAYER WARRIOR. I BELIEVE IN THE GOOD. I AM FAITHFUL.

I AM (fill in your blank)

_____

Prayer: Heavenly Father, I confess that I am a sinner in need of a Savior; thank You, Lord, for placing people in my life that will pray with me and for me. I know the power of prayer; it changes lives, it changes nations! Lord, let my prayer not be redundant or a habit; let me seek true connection with the Holy Spirit power living in me. I crave You. Lord. In Jesus' name, amen.

Thoughts/Notes/Encouragement/Inspiration:

_____

_____

_____

_____

_____

_____

DAY 53

Story: You can feed all the homeless people you want to, but if you don't have Jesus, you won't get heaven. All the money in the world can't buy salvation and all the good works and good deeds won't get you a free pass. There is NOTHING you can do to earn it; it is a GIFT, handed to you by the grace of the Almighty. Does that FIRE YOU UP?! I hope so! That means that no matter how many times you mess up, which if you're like me, it's about 50 times a day, His grace covers you. Now let me be clear; scripture says we are to conform to the life of Christ. We are to be more like Him in every way, but that doesn't mean perfect, that means doing our best to love and live as He has called. We will mess up. We will fall short. Then His grace will step in and cover us. He will hold you up with His righteous right hand. I keep saying it because it's true, He doesn't need you to be "perfect' or "have it all together," He needs you to obey His call to serve, however that looks for you. Baptism is the symbol of faith that you show to those around you, so they know you're "set apart." Baptism doesn't save you, all it takes is a simple confession of your lips; "I am a sinner, I believe that Jesus Christ died and rose on the third day." BAM! That's it; did you pray that prayer for the first time? Welcome to the FAMILY! Be sure to reach out to someone in your home church to talk about what it means to be a new believer. Get a Bible; start reading and praying over it. Ask God to reveal His truth to you through His Word. Now walk in the truth that your life matters and you're called to make disciples and share the good things He has done for you.

Verse: Titus 3:5-6

"He saved us not because of the righteous things we have done, but because of His mercy. He saved us through the washing of rebirth and renewal by the Holy Spirit."

~~(Un)~~ Forgiven

Scripture Application: Read the verse in its context. How will you apply the message of this verse to your life today?

_____

_____

Gratitude:

_____

_____

Affirmations: I AM LIGHT. I AM (fill in your blank)

_____

Prayer: Heavenly Father, thank You that heaven doesn't require good works. Thank You that we get to serve and love others because You call us to, not as a qualification to get into heaven. You came down from heaven, born in the humblest of circumstances, and lived to die a gruesome death for me. And all You ask is that I love You and live for You. It is the best gift I have ever been given, and thank You that I get to share Your good news today. I know I fall short daily and that Your grace is there when I need it. Let me never stop shining a light for You, no matter my circumstances. In Jesus' name, amen.

Thoughts/Notes/Encouragement/Inspiration:

_____

_____

_____

DAY 54

Story: Nothing you've done is hidden from God. He knows the worst parts of you and still loves you unconditionally. He knew every struggle you'd face before the creation of the world, and He still thought you worthy of being here. He sees you, every part of you, and He calls you worthy. In your mess and your struggle, He sees you and He loves you. Have you ever felt disconnected from God? You know He's there, but you can't quite figure out how to reach Him? You feel you've been away for too long? Lean in, stay in prayer; the devil doesn't want you in contact with God so if you feel the pull to avoid prayer, lean in. Stay in the Word, the guidebook of life. Every solution to every problem is there, waiting for you. Let His Word sink into the depths of your soul; it will pull you out of the pit. There is nowhere you can run where you are out of His grace. He loves you; He needs you to know that with a simple prayer, you can come home. He is waiting with open arms.

Verse: Hebrews 4:12-13

"For the Word of God is living and active. Sharper than any double-edged sword, it penetrates even to dividing soul and spirit, joint and marrow; it judges the thoughts and attitudes of the heart. Nothing in all creation is hidden from God's sight."

Scripture Application: Read the verse in its context. How will you apply the message of this verse to your life today?

_____

_____

_____

_____

~~(Un)~~ Forgiven

Gratitude:

_____

_____

Affirmations: I AM (fill in your blank)

_____

Prayer: Heavenly Father, I know You see me better than I see myself. You know my heart and the struggles I face; You know me better than I know myself. Thank You that I am changed by Your Word, thank you that 2,000+ years later Your Word is still alive and speaking to me. Let me immerse myself in who You are, Lord, so that I can be changed and transformed into the person You want me to be. In Jesus' name, amen.

Thoughts/Notes/Encouragement/Inspiration:

_____

_____

_____

_____

_____

_____

DAY 55

Story: The closer I draw to God the sneakier the enemy gets. It used to come in food and alcohol; today it comes in fear of not doing all I'm supposed to or worry over my business or having a baby. The enemy is sneaky, and he hates us. Scripture tells us "he prowls around like a lion looking for someone to devour." (1 Peter 5:8) He loves to fill us with doubt, distraction and delay or procrastination; these are all part of his schemes. He has an army of evil cohorts who constantly try to bring shame or fear into our lives. James 4:7 says, "submit yourselves to God, resist the devil and he will flee." Cast him OUT of your life, your head and your home. Learn to recognize the still small voice of Holy Spirit conviction and the lie of the enemy. Good = God, anything else, cast it out! You are a child of the Most High God! Shout it to the rooftops and watch evil flee from your home. The gate, in the context of this verse, is small, a narrow gate, not everyone will enter, but let's try, let's share the Word and shine light on the gospel and tell of the wonderful, glorious things He has done! He's changed your life; don't you want everyone to experience this freedom? If you're too afraid of the judgement of others, you need to take that to the foot of the cross. Do you fear others' opinions or facing God at the end of your life? Don't keep the good news to yourself! Write below one person you can share with today.

Verse: John 10:9

"I am the gate, whoever enters through me will be saved."

Scripture Application: Read the verse in its context. How will you apply the message of this verse to your life today?

_____

_____

_____

~~(Un)~~ Forgiven

Gratitude:

_____

_____

Affirmation: I AM SAVED. I AM HOLY. I AM BLESSED. I AM (fill in your blank)

_____

Prayer: Heavenly Father, we know that the only way to heaven is through You. Show me how I can share Your love with everyone I meet today, either in a compliment or passing smile; let the light of Jesus shine through me so that the gate to enter heaven is crowded. I know not everyone will enter heaven's gate, Lord, but I want to share the light of Jesus with those that will listen. In Jesus' name, amen.

Thoughts/Notes/Encouragement/Inspiration:

_____

_____

_____

_____

_____

DAY 56

Story: Not everyone goes to heaven. I hope that breaks your heart like it does mine. We know from the Word that this is the truth. God loves us so much that He came to Earth as a baby, He lived a normal life as a normal boy who grew to be a man who lived sinless, who would die and rise to life, proving His love for us. He would show the world and those who choose to believe who He is. His love is the best gift we will ever receive: salvation through the blood offered on the cross by the only perfect Man who has ever existed. I want everyone I love to experience the awe and wonder of the love of God, and I suspect that you do too. How can we love people and share the good news of the cross in a way that brings honor to Him? How can we show people through the way we love them that our only hope of heaven and salvation comes through Jesus Christ? As believers we MUST share. When people ask why we're happy in our lowest times, do you feel confident in telling them why? Seek His face in those moments; a simple "Lord, give me the words" will allow His Spirit to speak through you. Prayerfully come up with a phrase using His words that will allow you, over time, to share the message of His love. He will give you the words; you just need to pray for the courage to speak them.

Verse: 1 John 3:1

"How great is the love the Father has lavished on us, that we should be called children of God."

Scripture Application: Read the verse in its context. How will you apply the message of this verse to your life today?

_____

_____

_____

~~(Un)~~ Forgiven

Gratitude:

_____

_____

Affirmations: I AM LOVED. I AM CHOSEN. I AM (fill in your blank)

_____

Prayer: Heavenly Father, thank You that I am a child of God! You call me chosen, in Your precious name! Thank You, Lord, for thinking me worthy enough to create; let me never take it for granted. Father, I want to always do Your will! In Jesus' name, amen.

Thoughts/Notes/Encouragement/Inspiration:

_____

_____

_____

_____

_____

_____

DAY 57

Story: Do you worry about how you're being served at a restaurant instead of how you can serve others? Do you find yourself always looking for what you can get from someone or what you can give to someone? Jesus washed the disciples' feet KNOWING that Judas would betray Him and Peter would deny Him, not once, but THREE TIMES. He washed their feet anyway. You were not put on this earth to be served but to serve, and the entitlement we often feel has got to be changed. Every day I would like to challenge you to say, "Okay, Lord, who can I serve and how can I serve today?" How can you make your spouse's life better today? How can you be a better employee or coworker to the person who drives you crazy and is always negative? We don't always have to go somewhere to serve; yes, we should do that as well, but learning to serve your spouse instead of worrying how they're not serving you is a great place to start. God gave His life so we could share His good news. We constantly see commercials on what we can buy for ourselves that we probably don't need or things we can eat that we probably shouldn't. It's about serving self instead of serving others. How can you better serve those around you today? Any ideas how you can step out of your comfort bubble to serve in the way God is calling you?

Verse: Matthew 20:28

"Just as the Son of Man did not come to be served, but to serve and to give His life as the ransom for many."

Scripture Application: Read the verse in its context. How will you apply the message of this verse to your life today?

_____

_____

_____

~~(Un)~~ Forgiven

Gratitude:

_____

_____

Affirmations: I AM CHANGED. I AM A SERVANT. I AM (fill in your blank)

_____

Prayer: Heavenly Father, I want to serve, I want to be obedient to the call and purpose You've placed on my life. Show me what that looks like for me, I want to step into divine purpose today so that I can bring glory and honor to You every day of my life! Lead me, Lord; let my life be a living sacrifice to You! In Jesus' name, amen.

Thoughts/Notes/Encouragement/Inspiration:

_____

_____

_____

_____

_____

_____

DAY 58

Story: When Jesus gave the Great Commission, He called us to make disciples of ALL nations. How are we supposed to do that when often our greatest sphere of influence is our social media? Maybe He's calling you to look closer to home. When we disciple our children, their faith spreads. When we come alongside others who are hungry for more, their faith spreads like wildfire. When we share our testimony with people in our lives, they relate to us, they see that there is healing in the cross, they are saved, and their faith spreads like wildfire. Do you SEE what happens here? Your story matters. I hope it doesn't hold trauma like mine; maybe it does, maybe it doesn't. Either way, you have a story and to someone who aches to be in the place you are, wherever that may be, they need to hear that there IS victory in struggle. When we operate in good faith as Jesus calls us to, when our life is the example of His grace and mercy, lives ARE changed. Stop downplaying your story because you don't feel like it's enough or too much. Someone somewhere needs to know that there IS hope. Don't rely on your strength to share, ask God to give you the words you need to connect the way you need to connect. He won't ask you to come up with the words to say, He will provide them. He just needs you to be obedient and to act.

Verse: 1 Timothy 1:5

"The goal of this command is love, which comes from a pure heart, a good conscience and a sincere faith."

Scripture Application: Read the verse in its context. How will you apply the message of this verse to your life today?

_____

_____

_____

~~(Un)~~ Forgiven

Gratitude:

_____

_____

Affirmations: I AM LIGHT. I AM (fill in your blank)

_____

Prayer: Heavenly Father, I want to love like You. I want to shine Your light everywhere I go. Lead me, Lord; help me to see in me what You see. I know I am unqualified, but I know You have called. I am ready to step into the truth of Your purpose in my life today. Show me how I can love those You've called me to love and disciple those You've called me to disciple. Create in me a clean heart so I can live out my calling in Your name. Amen.

Thoughts/Notes/Encouragement/Inspiration:

_____

_____

_____

_____

_____

DAY 59

Story: Do you want a white stone? Do you want your name to be written in the "Lamb's book of life" as Dr. Charles Stanley would say? Do you want your name to be written in heaven? Repent of your sin and ask God to heal your broken heart. Jesus did die, He DID rise from the dead. Did you know that the account of the resurrection was proven by atheists? Did you know that over 500 people saw Jesus after His resurrection? We teach evolution in schools, but the proof of creation exists, as opposed to monkeys becoming men. God has hidden manna for you, too. He gives us everything we actually need in scripture; He gives us everything we need through Holy Spirit connection but it's on us to cultivate our faith, so it speaks in a voice that is loud and loving to the people we meet. Do you know how to talk to people about God? One thing I've felt convicted about is just asking questions. I do this with clients too. Ask questions; get to know people. Oftentimes it opens conversations up to many interesting topics and what's more interesting than sharing your testimony? Sharing IS caring and who knows, you may inspire someone to go on their own quest for salvation. Isn't that the point?

Verse: Revelation 2:17

"He who has an ear, let him hear what the Spirit says to the churches. To him who overcomes I will give some of the hidden manna. I will also give him a white stone with a new name written on it, known only to him who receives it."

Scripture Application: Read the verse in its context. How will you apply the message of this verse to your life today?

_____

_____

_____

~~(Un)~~ Forgiven

Gratitude:

_____

_____

Affirmations I AM (fill in your blank)

_____

Prayer: Heavenly Father, I don't always know what to say or do. I don't always know the questions to ask. I don't understand what Revelation means and I ask that you clarify it for me; show me what you need me to see, Lord. Let my eyes and ears and heart be open to You and the message of scripture, then help me apply it to my life today. I don't want to go through the motions of my faith, I want to be intentional in my relationship with You; show me how. In Jesus' name, amen.

Thoughts/Notes/Encouragement/Inspiration:

_____

_____

_____

_____

_____

DAY 60

Story: I hear too often "Come back, Jesus" and while yes, heaven is a treasure awaiting us, I have far too many loved ones that don't have salvation. When we accept Christ as our Savior we are to conform to His image, we are to live as He calls us, to love people and make disciples. It is selfish of us to have freedom in Christ and not share it with everyone we meet. Not in a preachy type of way, but just acknowledgement of His presence in our lives. When someone asks why you're smiling in the "pit," you can say "Because I know God will use it for His glory, He has before." Or when someone praises you for a job well done when you KNOW it was Holy Spirit-driven, you can say "Yes! I love it when God uses me this way." Simple acknowledgement of His guidance and presence in your life will go a lot farther than preaching to someone who isn't ready to accept Him. Do you have a simple phrase or two you can use that gives God the glory in your life? How do you shine the light of Jesus to a non-believer in a non-preachy way? In that moment say, "Lord, give me the words." I do this ALL THE TIME!

Verse: 2 Peter 3:14

"So, then dear friends, since you are looking forward to this, make every effort to be found guiltless, blameless and at peace with Him."

Scripture Application: Read the verse in its context. How will you apply the message of this verse to your life today?

_____

_____

_____

_____

~~(Un)~~ Forgiven

Gratitude:

_____

_____

Affirmations: I AM (fill in your blank)

_____

Prayer: Heavenly Father, I long for Your arrival but I don't want to sit idly waiting. I know that only YOU know when the time is here. I want to love people to discipleship in the meantime. Lord, I don't always know what to say to a non-believer; please use my voice to share in those times. I want everyone to have the freedom in You that I have. In Jesus' name, amen.

Thoughts/Notes/Encouragement/Inspiration:

_____

_____

_____

_____

_____

_____

A Final Thought and Call to Action

As we close, please consider that, in the Old Testament, God's people had to travel to the tabernacle to atone for their sins. If you've ever read the Bible or heard of the Tabernacle of Meeting or Tent of Meeting, that's what they mean. God would come down and the people would travel with their animals to make sacrifices to atone for their sins. Hubs and I are reading Numbers now, and it's talking a lot about the different types of sacrifices required and all the numbers of different kinds of animals for which type of sacrifice, etc. To be honest, I don't know how they kept it all straight. If you've not read the Bible, I highly suggest you do. It's a lot, and much of it I struggle to understand; I pray over it and ask God to reveal to me what I need to learn. Okay, so fast forward thousands of years later, AFTER the death of Christ. Jesus kept talking through His ministry about atoning for our sins and that He came to reign with God. He kept talking about the perfect sacrifice that would remove the rules and law of Moses that once was in force. People thought He was coming to take a physical seat at the throne of Rome, which goes to show us how we often limit God's power in our lives. Anyway, so Christ is crucified and raised to life after three days. He then walked the earth for 50 days; we call this Pentecost. He wanted to make sure that there were plenty of witnesses that would see Him and recall His resurrection. Many people today still question Jesus' resurrection and many people have gone on to try disprove it completely. Have you heard of *The Case for Christ?* This is a book written by Lee Strobel, an atheist whose wife was saved after their daughter nearly died. Strobel went on a three-year mission to disprove the resurrection of Christ and at the end of his search he ended up getting saved. He became a pastor and helps people find the truth of the gospel he found. For centuries,

~~(Un)~~ Forgiven

atheists have tried to disprove Christ's resurrection and most of them end up becoming believers themselves. Remind you of anyone? Paul, formerly Saul, on the road to Damascus, maybe? Okay, so back to my original point. So, Jesus lives for 50 days on the earth and is then taken up on a cloud to be seated at the right hand of the Father. In that moment, we read that He "sends a helper" in the Holy Spirit. Okay, but what does that mean? Remember above when I talked about the Israelites having to travel to the temple to meet with God? Well, when Jesus ascended and He sent the Holy Spirit to dwell in us when we ask Christ to lead our lives, it means that Jesus lives IN us… Yes, the living God lives inside us. He is with us always. We can repent to Him any time we need to instead of having to travel to a tent with our 40 sheep and goats (insert laugh here), but most importantly, in my opinion, He will guide us, lead us and direct us when we seek Him. The power of the Holy Spirit is something I think many believers don't always grasp. We try to do life on our own, go our own way, even when we've asked Him to be Lord over our lives. But in a moment, we can redirect our thoughts and seek His will above our own. The fruits of the Spirit we've read about already are found in Galatians, and when we ask God to lead our lives and He comes to live IN us, this is why we say we have the fruits He has, because He lives in us. The same power that Jesus had on the cross, the same power He had when He rose from the dead, lives IN us. It's sometimes unfathomable, isn't it? It is to me. I've learned to seek His will over and over, day after day, choice after choice. Of course, my flesh kicks in and I wobble and sin and fall short, but He's there to scoop me up and remind me that "when I am weak, He is strong." Do you consult the Holy Spirit in all things in your life? Maybe you do, maybe not. Maybe your intentions are there but your flesh kicks in like mine. Either way, I encourage you to wake up with Him daily and ask Him to fill you with His Spirit, so that, when life happens and a split-second decision is to be made, He is the one tapping you on your shoulder, leading you in the right direction. This gift is powerful and one you can and should cultivate, because when God leads your life is better. When we trust Him, life is better. When we know that our power lies with Him, the One who created all things, the One who conquered death, the One who thought you worthy of creation, the One who will forgive your sins and lead you to everlasting life, the One who loves you more than anyone. When we can rest our faith upon that, we become more and more like Him, and in those moments of doubt or fear or insecurity we can find peace knowing that we are (~~un~~)*forgiven*, we are loved, we are His, we always were, we always will be, and that is a mighty safe place to be.

I would like to invite you to join my Free Online Community. Visit me at <u>www.lindyschlabach.com</u>, enter your email, and I'll send you the link to my Free Community where I do free monthly challenges to help you reach your fitness and nutrition goals in a Godly way. I'll also send you a copy of my Faith-Inspired Habit & Nutrition Planner that will help you align your goals and break chains with God. Follow me on Instagram and Facebook at Lindy Schlabach Fitness. I look forward to getting to know you!

Appendix

I highly recommend *Miracle Morning* by Hal Elrod if you struggle to get up in the mornings, as well as *5 Second Rule* by Mel Robbins.

If you struggle with food, Lysa Terkeurst's *Made to Crave 60 Day Devotional* is so helpful! I read and re-read it 11 times in a row! Reference Devotional Day 52.

Dr. Charles Stanley at In Touch Ministries created a legacy for every believer. His YouTube channel is my Sunday morning go-to while we get ready for church.

Joyce Meyer and her no-nonsense testimony is one I relate to well. Her *Battlefield of the Mind* book is one I think of often.

Page 13- *Breaking Free* by Beth Moore

Page 41- *Fail Forward* John C. Maxwell

Page 105 Lee Strobel's *The Case for Christ*

All Bible verses in this text come from the NLT (New Living Translation)

Page 16- Corinthians 10:5

Page 18- John 16:33 and Isaiah 55:8

Page 20- Matthew 18:20

Page 24- Joyce Meyer sermon on YouTube

Page 25- Reference Jesus Calling

Page 27- Galatians 6:9

Page 34- Reference the YouVersion app

Page 35- Ephesians 3:20

Page 40- Fasting references in Luke 4 and 18, Matthew 6, and Zachariah

Page 42- John 19:30

Page 44- Psalm 139:23-24

~~(Un)~~ Forgiven

Notes

One to three goals at a time; write them down in a journal. I like the $5 journals from the Dollar General; there are so many great options!

One to three steps you can take TODAY to work towards your goals, whatever they may be. Then be intentional about reaching them and give yourself grace when they fall apart. I tell clients, if you get one day a week that's a 10/10, celebrate, because most days will be about average. Grace over grind and OBEDIENCE over outcome. Let God lead your choices and you will always win!

Read and re-read these scriptures; they will apply differently to your life at different times. The Bible always applies to daily life; it is the best tool you have to live a joy filled life, even in the times of struggle.

Bible Verse:

Goals:

    1.

    2.

    3.

Steps TODAY:

    1.

    2.

3.

This goal is important to me because when I accomplish it I will be:

_____

Thank You, Lord, for the opportunity to honor You with my choices!

~~(Un)~~ Forgiven

About the Author

Lindy Schlabach was born and raised in Northeast Indiana. She is the wife of Darrel and dog mom to Dory. She and her husband are on the journey to grow their family. She is an avid reader and lover of the lake and her family. Lindy hopes to write many books through her life, sharing her testimony and how God's love and grace continues to meet her each day, in the good, the bad and in between.

Lindy graduated from Anderson University in 2004 with a Bachelor's degree. She loves to cook with her hubby, go for walks with her dog, and loves to garden and take naps. She's usually carrying a snack in her purse and loves coffee, dark chocolate, and road trips with Darrel.

She lives in a small town in Indiana on a chain of lakes and looks forward to spending time with friends and family on their boat in the summer.

Postscript: P.S.

This isn't the end of our story; our next chapter is only the beginning. From heartache and infertility to a journey of healing and restoration; the good, bad, overwhelming and the blessings. May this journey be yet another reflection of God's perfect plan for this imperfect life and how God's grace continues to shower us through this journey of healing and restoration. If your life isn't good, He isn't done. Hold tight to your dreams; you're only one answered prayer away.

Lindy Schlabach

Printed in the USA
CPSIA information can be obtained
at www.ICGtesting.com
LVHW021133191024
794268LV00001B/49